Hoswick Man

Hoswick Man

Martin Smith

*Memories in words and pictures of his family
and his early years growing up in
Hoswick, Sandwick, Shetland.*

The Shetland Times
Lerwick
2011

Hoswick Man

First published by The Shetland Times Ltd., 2011.

Copyright © Wills Martin Smith, 2011.

ISBN 978-1-904746-69-0

All rights reserved.
No part of this publication may be reproduced, stored in a retrieval system, or transmitted, in any form, or by any means, electronic, mechanical, photocopying, recording or otherwise, without the prior written permission of the publishers.

Wills Martin Smith has asserted his rights under the Copyright, Designs and Patents Act, 1988, to be identified as the author of this work.

British Library Cataloguing-in-Publication Data
A catalogue record for this book is available from the British Library

Printed and published by
The Shetland Times Ltd.,
Gremista, Lerwick,
Shetland, Scotland. ZE1 0PX

*I dedicate this book to my parents,
Willie and Adeline Smith (née Ewenson),
whose love and commitment, hard work
and personal sacrifices gave me
such a wonderful start in life.*

Contents

Acknowledgements ix
Introduction xi
Great-grandparents 1
Grandparents Sandwick 9
Grandparents Sand 25
Coming Together 36
Making Ends Meet 54
Entertainment and Hobbies 59
Aggie and Jean Harper 66
Harold (Frank) Mathews 70
Learning to Cycle 78
Christmas and New Year 80
Beachcombing 82
Going to School 85
The Sandwick Baking Company (The Bakeshop) Fire 90
Local Amenities 93
Sunday 96
School Holidays 100
The Van Men 108
A New Beginning 117
The Commercial Course 125
Appendices 130

Acknowledgements

I would like to express my thanks to the following for their help in the production of this book:

Edna Burke, former manageress of the Shetland Times Bookshop, for encouraging me to write it.

Sandwick History Group.

The staff of Shetland Archives for their help and assistance during my many visits.

My aunt, Jean Isbister, for the family history and the home bakes!

My cousin, Ian Isbister, and his wife Eunice.

My cousin, Ronnie Mouat.

Charlotte Black and The Shetland Times Ltd. for agreeing to publish it.

The staff of The Shetland Times Ltd for the excellent job they have done of turning my typed notes and scanned photographs into such an excellent book.

The people of Sandwick and Hoswick who, during conversations over many years, triggered memories that have found their way into this book.

Introduction

I have toyed with the idea of writing a book about my family and my early life growing up in Hoswick, Sandwick for a number of years.

I knew that my Sandwick grandparents had a large collection of photographs because I used to be shown them when I was a boy. *(If only I had had the means of recording the details then that I have now.)* However, I wasn't sure how many had survived their various moves or the clearing out of their house after they passed away.

Several boxes spent many years in my father's garage at Lochside, Lerwick, and, after he died, many more in mine.

It was only after I retired in May 2007 and began to look through the various boxes that I realised just how much material there was. To date, I have scanned into my computer system well over 2,000 items including birth and death certificates, passports, references, private letters, invoices, telegrams and several hundred photographs.

In addition to this treasure trove, I also had several hundred photographs taken by my father in the 1940s, 1950s and early 1960s, as well as other items kept by my mother.

Reading through some of the papers it soon became clear just how hard the lives of my grandparents and great-grandparents had been. The lives of my parents, although better in many respects, hadn't been a bed of roses either.

I decided that, if for no reason other than as a historical record, I would use the information together with my own memories and photographs to put together this book about my family and my early years.

Compiling the book has been a very interesting and at times educational experience. Along the way I have discovered many more things about my family and the times in which they lived than I already knew.

I have enjoyed the experience. I hope you will too.

Wills Martin Smith

Great-grandparents

Magnus Smith was born on 11th October, 1876, at Stove, Sandwick, one of a family of ten. His father was Oliver Smith (fisherman), and his mother Elizabeth Smith (nee Work). He would have gone to the Sandwick School and left at the age of 14. I don't know if he went into the blacksmith trade straight from school but that is what he is best known for throughout Sandwick.

Magnus Smith (Smiddy Magnie) outside the Smithy at Central, Sandwick. Photographer unknown.

On 20th October, 1900, he wrote to the laird asking for land on which to build a smithy. He received the following reply from the laird at the Sumburgh Estate office on the 22nd:

> Dear Sir,
>
> I have received your letter of the 20th inst. but I cannot give you a final answer without having a talk with you. Come and see me the next time I am at Sandlodge and I will see what can be done for you.
>
> It is not wise to set a man down where he cannot make a decent living. Now there are at present two Blacksmith's shops in Sandwick Parish, and it comes to be a question if there is trade enough to keep a third one.
>
> Meanwhile I would suggest for your consideration what I think would be a very good opening for a Blacksmith, namely, Vidlin in Lunnasting. There is no Blacksmith in the Parish of Lunnasting and Nesting. There used to be a Blacksmith at Voe, Delting but there is none there now, and the people have to get their work done in Lerwick 25 miles away.
>
> Every encouragement would be given to a good Blacksmith setting up in the District.
>
> Think it over before I see you.
>
> Yours faithfully,
>
> John W Bruce

The well-meant advice from the laird wasn't heeded and Magnie went ahead with the smithy at the Central, Sandwick. However, just two years later, he writes to the laird again:

> Leebitton,
> Sandwick Parish,
> 16th Sept. 1902
>
> John Bruce Esq.,
> Sumburgh.
>
> Dear Sir,
>
> As I find to carry on the Blacksmith business at Central Smithy Sandwick and make a success of the same means an expenditure

that I don't see my way clear to risk; My Partner Matthew Sinclair is willing to take the responsibility providing you will grant the Feu in his own name.

This would suit me much better as I would still work in the place as before.

If you can see your way to grant the same and will kindly let us know what it will cost to have the Deed transferred we will make the necessary arrangements.

Trusting you will consider the matter and let me know as soon as possible.

I am Sir

Yours respectfully,

Magnus Smith

The request was duly granted by the laird and Magnie continued to work in the smiddy for several years before being called up to serve in the Great War. He must have returned to the smithy after the war and continued to work there until the 1920s.

From left: James Duncan, Andrina Smith (née Duncan), Chrissie Smith (Andrina's daughter), truck driver. Photographer unknown (possibly Willie Smith).

The firm of M. Smith & Co. appears in *Manson's Almanac* up until 1934, but from correspondence that I have, Magnie was working as a foreman for the roads department in 1927, when he would have been 51, so I don't know exactly when he ceased being a blacksmith.

Amongst some of his papers I found a faded invoice from M. Smith & Co. Next to the name on either side are two little boxes with the words 'Pony Ploughs a speciality' in one, and 'Boat Work got out at shortest notice' in the other – a measure of just how important the boats at Broonies Taing were for the local blacksmiths, three of whom were now working in Sandwick.

Andrina Thompson Duncan was born at Greenmow, Cunningsburgh, on 17th December, 1873, one of a family of four. She was the only one of my great-grandparents still alive when I was born. Her father was Malcolm Duncan and her mother Christina Thomson. I have no knowledge of where she went to school but I do remember her telling me all about working with the herring at Broonies Taing and how she had to wrap her fingers up with strips of cloth before she went to work. In the winter time she mended herring nets for various boats so that they were ready for the start of the next season.

Andrina and Magnus Smith were married on 14th April, 1898, at Fleet Street, Lerwick. They set up home at Leebotten and had one daughter, Chrissie.

When Andrina was just six years old, her father, Malcolm, had an accident in the Sandlodge copper mine, on 4th September, 1879. The injuries that he sustained were so severe that he had to have *both* his hands amputated. (There is an excellent account of the accident in Wendy Gear's book, *John Walker's Shetland*.)

From the time of his accident until his death, Malcolm Duncan was known as Hookie Maikie, owing to the fact that he had hooks instead of hands. The prostheses that he used were made for him by Magnus Smith (Smiddy Magnie) and were made in such a way that a fork, knife and spoon could be screwed into the prosthesis, allowing Maikie to eat normally. They were still in Rocklea when I was a small boy but, unfortunately, were dumped when my parents cleaned out the Rocklea house after my grandparents' death.

Having someone with such a serious disability in the 1880s must have made life very hard for the Duncan family.

In 1907, Magnus Smith asked the laird for a piece of land on which to build a house. On 30th January, 1908, a feu was set off at a cost of £2 per annum, plus eight shillings (40p) for the land adjoining it on which to grow crops.

Andrina Smith fetching water from the Milton well. The author tried carrying water using the same yoke some 30+ years later. Photographer unknown.

The stones for the house came from a small outcrop of rock to the east of the old Sandwick school building and were taken to the building site by horse and gig. The stones were all flat and would have been very easy for the masons to build with. The house was finished in 1912 and named Rocklea.

When she was in her forties, Andrina had an illness that resulted in her losing all her hair. She also suffered from poor eyesight for a number of years before going completely blind in 1948.

The Church of Scotland played a big part in the lives of Magnie and Andrina who were both members of the congregation and the choir there for many years.

Magnie died in 1944, aged 68, and Andrina in 1960, at the age of 86.

Rocklea Cottage, Stove, Sandwick, built for Magnus Smith (Smiddy Magnie).
Photo: Willie Smith

GREAT-GRANDPARENTS 7

Above: Magnus and Andrina Smith sitting in their garden at Rocklea, Stove, Sandwick, probably on a Sunday. Note 'Milton' house in background and new peats built on to the old stacks..

Below: Andrina Smith (née Duncan) and her husband Magnus Smith (Smiddy Magnie) cutting corn on the rigs next to Rocklea, Stove, Sandwick.

(Jimmy) James Duncan (left); ?; ?; Andrina Smith; ?; Jeannie Duncan with kishie.

Grandparents Sandwick

William Smith, or, as he was better known, Willie a' Milton, was born on 1st November, 1893, at Milltown (Milton), Stove, Sandwick, one of a family of six. He went to the local Sandwick School and on leaving went to work for the Laird at Sandlodge.

He worked there for several years until he was called to serve his King and country in the First World War. On 8th November, 1915, aged 22, he joined the Royal Naval Reserve and immediately became part of the Mobilised Naval Service serving on several ships including HMS *Ariadne* for initial training, before being transferred to the destroyer HMS *Resolution*.

Willie a' Milton in his naval uniform. The cap ribbon reads HMS Resolution. *His wife to be, Chrissie Smith, is on his right.*
Photo: R. H. Ramsay

10   HOSWICK MAN

Above: Tommy Smith (left) and Stanley 'Milton' Sothcott, taken at Milltown (Milton) Sandwick. Photographer unknown.

Left: Joan Smith, Mother of William Smith (Willie a' Milton). **Photo: R. H. Ramsay**

Below: Milton Cottage, Sandwick. Willie a' Milton's birthplace. Photographer unknown.

The 30,000-ton *Resolution* was built in 1915-16; she was armed with 2 x 3-inch anti-aircraft guns, 14 x 6-inch guns and 8 x 15-inch guns. Each of the 15-inch guns weighed 100 tons and could fire a 1938-pound shell 16¼ miles using a 490-pound cordite charge! One of these guns still survives and can be seen at the Imperial War Museum in London.

Above: *The destroyer, HMS* Resolution.

Below *This picture gives you a good idea what the business end of a 15-inch gun looks like.*

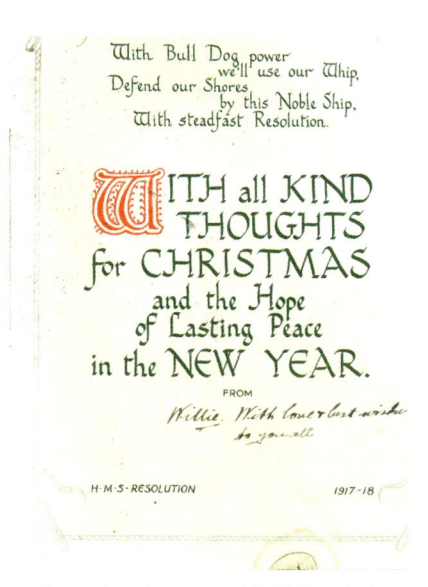

The front and inside of a Christmas card sent from the destroyer, HMS Resolution, *Christmas 1917. Note the wording.*

Resolution carried a crew of 920 men and saw service in both world wars before being scrapped in 1948.

She must have been an awesome sight to someone of Willie's background, age and experience.

It was whilst going through some of Willie's papers that I found his hand-written account of an operation HMS *Resolution* took part in that led to the destruction of two Zeppelin sheds.

> *Left Rosyth Tuesday night 12p.m. 16th July 1918 with Furious, Res. Rar. R. O. & R. S. For to make a raid at Schleswig – Holstein and bomb Zeppelin Sheds. Furious carrying air ships. (aeroplanes equipped with floats to allow them to land on water) Remainder of ships standing by in case of any Hun fleet coming out.*
>
> *Arrived in danger zone Thursday morning but owing to fog operations were delayed until Friday morning 3.30 (During delay fleet patrolled the course we had just come)*
>
> *Raid successfully carried out on Friday morning. Two Zeppelin sheds blown down and serious fires caused. Three pilots out of*

seven returned to Furious, believed some of the rest alighted in Denmark near to where the raid was carried out. Lots of mines sunk while at sea. Our subs were also out. Res nearly bumped one mine.

Friday forenoon started our journey back after waiting for Furious to join us with what air ships had returned to her.

Friday night 8 p.m. heard the destroyer Valentine had picked up the four pilots that did not return to Furious.

From the 31st October, 1918, to the 2nd March, 1919, he served in the trawler section of the Royal Naval Reserve as a deck hand. His naval service finally coming to an end on 7th November, 1920, six days after his 27th birthday.

Chrissie Smith, the only daughter of Magnus Smith (Smiddy Magnie) and Andrina Duncan, was born on 2nd August, 1898. She went to school in Sandwick and early on in life learned to play the organ. Music played a big part in her life for many years. She is listed in *Mansons' Almanac* in the mid-1920s as one of five music teachers in Sandwick.

A World War One Christmas card.

14 Hoswick Man

Chrissie and Willie a' Milton had courted for a number of years. On 2nd August, 1918 – her 20th birthday – he gave her a brooch which has the profile of HMS *Resolution* engraved on the front, surrounded by a belt and bearing the words 'Britain's Glory'; the rear is inscribed 'To Chrissie from Willie'. They were married on 30th December, 1920, setting up home in Hoswick.

The brooch given to Chrissie Smith on her 20th birthday. It is reputed to have been made by an engineer on board HMS Resolution *who, in peace time, was a jeweller in Edinburgh*

Just two days before their wedding they went shopping in Lerwick for some essential items. The following details have been taken from the actual invoices and retyped for the sake of clarity. Their total spend came to £21 10s 10d.

Johnson & Greig – Owners and Publishers of The Shetland Times

Dec 28th 1920	18 cake cards	£- 11s 6d
Dec 28th 1920	18 cake boxes	4s 6d
Dec 28th 1920	**Total**	**£- 16s 0d**

Smith & Robertson, Commercial Street, Lerwick

Dec 28th 1920	Tie		3s 9d
Dec 28th 1920	Socks		2s
Dec 28th 1920	Hat		9s 6d
Dec 28th 1920	Umbrella		14s 9d
Dec 28th 1920	2 Handkerchiefs @ 11d		1s 8d
Dec 28th 1920	Sub Total		£1 11s 8d
Dec 28th 1920	Less returns gloves	10s 6d	
Dec 28th 1920	Less returns Tie	5s	
Dec 28th 1920	**Total**		**£- 16s 2d**

GRANDPARENTS SANDWICK 15

William Smith (Willie a' Milton) and Chrissie Smith, Rocklea, Stove, on their wedding day.
Photo: R. H. Ramsay

Stove and Smith, Commercial Street, Lerwick

Dec 28th 1920 1 Pair Straw Palliassis (Mattresses)	£1 4s 6d
Dec 28th 1920 2 Wool Pillows	13s
Dec 28th 1920 1 6ft x 3ft 6 wool bolster	12s 9d
Dec 28th 1920 **Total**	**£2 10s 3d**

Malcolm Duncan, Joiner and Undertaker, South Hillhead, Lerwick

Dec 28th 1920 Cash for Bed 6ft x 3ft 6	**£5 0s 0d**

Taylor & Blance

Dec 28th 1920 1 Brides Cake	£3 10s 0d
Dec 28th 1920 Flowers	£0 6s 8d
Dec 28th 1920 **Total**	**£3 16s 8d**

John Linklater, Bank Lane, Lerwick.

Dec 28th 1920 1 Gents Suit	**£8 11s 9d**

After the Great War, Willie a' Milton worked in the Sandlodge Copper Mine before leaving Shetland, his wife, and infant son, on 12th May, 1922, to go and find work in New Zealand. The following is his account of the voyage there on board the 9,300-ton steamship, *Arawa*:

Workers at the Sandlodge mine. Photographer unknown.

Willie a' Milton sent this postcard of the steamer Arawa to his wife at Rocklea just hours before he sailed on her to New Zealand. On the back he wrote: 'Southampton May 18th. Sailing sometime today not sure when. Lovely weather hope you have got the same. A good crowd of passengers going so I think we will have a good time. Love to all WS XX'. **Photo: Kingston Real Photo Series**

> Sailed from Southampton in the afternoon of the 18th May, 1922
> Got to Colon on the night of June 3rd at 9.30
> First land sighted after leaving England was West India Islands
> Took on coal at Colon on Sunday Morning (100 tons in 8 minutes!)
> Started through the canal at noon on Sunday and took seven hours to go through
> Stopped at Balboa on Sunday night and went ashore
> Left Balboa again on Monday June 5th
> Crossed the line (equator) on 7th June during the night
> Sighted and passed Galapagos Islands on Thursday 8th June
> ARAWA June 10th 1922 Penton Harris infant son of Elsie Harris died and was buried at sea.
> June 17th 1922 Passed two small islands near Pitcairn Island
> June 17th 1922 Fancy dress ball aboard ARAWA
> June 29th1922 Arrived Wellington New Zealand (Left Home May 12th 1922)
> Left Wellington 4th July 1922 8.20 a.m.
> Arrived Hawera July 4th1922 at 6 p.m.

18   Hoswick Man

Above: Willie a' Milton (sitting on tree with pipe) and the rest of the sawmill workers. Photographer unknown.

Left: Willie a' Milton (right) and two of his mates having a few beers after a day's fishing. Location: Te-Kiri. Photographer unknown.

Below: Willie a' Milton in the doorway of his New Zealand hut, or Whare, Opanake. Photographer unknown.

Having breakfast in the hut. Note the bunk beds behind his head. Photographer unknown.

In the same small faded green notebook in which he recorded the above, I also found details of some of the places where he worked from August 1922 to July 1927:

> *Signed on Railway Works at Kapuni Aug 9th 1922*
> *Arrived Bradford's Farm Aug 10th*
> *Started work Aug 15th 1922*
> *Left Bradford's Farm Aug 3rd 1923*
> *Arrived Ornera Stream Aug 3rd 1923*
> *Started work on Mangowhera Bridge Aug 6th 1923*
> *Finished Mangowhera Bridge Nov 19th 1923*
> *Shipped to Patiki on Nov 28th 1923*
> *Shipped from Patiki to Opunake Dec 5th 1923*
> *Finished P. W. D. 8th Feb 1924*
> *Started Opunake C. C. Feb 19th 1924*
> *Finished E. C. C. Aug 22nd 1924*
>
> *Started TerKiri Mill Aug 24th 1924*
> *Two months off work*
> *One month Opunake harbour*
> *Started Orapuni July 13th 1927*

Unfortunately, I have not found any details of his employment from 1927 until he left New Zealand on 7th April, 1937, a passenger on board the RMS *Rangitata*, from Wellington to London via the Panama Canal. No hand-written diary of this trip, instead there is a booklet containing details of the ship, her crew, and a complete passenger list, parts of which can be found in the appendix.

In the back of the booklet space was provided for a log of the journey. Willie a' Milton kept this up to date daily throughout the journey; it is reproduced in the appendix so that those of you with a liking for such things can plot the course, speed and distance of his journey back to London, where he arrived on 10th May, 1937.

This little reminder of what he had left behind was also found in his notebook:

> *Give me a life in the dear old bush*
> *away from Civilisation*
> *Away from the bustle of the noisy crowd and*
> *the roar of the railway station*
>
> *We don't need a telephone to call up a pal*
> *to join in a rare old spree*
> *When we want a mate, his hand to shake*
> *we just give him a loud COO-EE*
>
> *author unknown*

Having arrived back home, Willie a' Milton got a job in the Scalloway quarry.

He also served in the Shetland Defence Battalion 10th Gordon's from 2nd September, 1939, until 31st May, 1941. I remember him telling me that there was an observation post on top of the Wester Quarff hill, from where he and his colleagues spent many hours keeping an eye out for any enemy activity. He said that with the binoculars they had up there it was possible to see the hens walking around the doors in Whalsay!

His employment at the Scalloway quarry ended in 1950 when, on 28th October that year, he became postman No. 57 for the east side of the Sandwick district. On the same day he started a diary in which he kept a record of each day's weather, road conditions, if the mail was late, the number of bags of mail, the amount of money collected for C.O.D. (cash on delivery) parcels, and any significant event happening in the district. He

Grandparents Sandwick   21

William Smith 'Willie Postie' in his postal uniform.   ***Photo: Willie Smith***

also recorded the Christmas 'presents' given to him by the generous people of his postal round on Christmas day. One year this amounted to £12 6/6 which must have been almost two weeks wages at the time.

In addition to his job as postman he was caretaker of the Carnegie Hall for several years. Every event that took place in the hall during this time is recorded, together with details of the films shown by Geordie Horne (Highlands and Islands Film Guild) and the number of books taken out from the library. The book is a truly remarkable record of life in Sandwick at the time and is far too long and detailed to be reproduced here in its entirety. Extensive extracts can be found in the appendix.

Willie a' Milton's time as postman in Sandwick came to an end on 31st October, 1959. Tom Halcrow took up a collection from the people in his postal district, and a social evening was arranged for Willie and his wife in the Central Hall, during which a complimentary speech was made by Mr Peter Tait and a wallet of notes presented by Miss Sylvia Leask. The evening's entertainment included a song by Miss Patsy Bray – *The Isles of Gletness* written by John Barclay. I have been told that this may have been the first public performance of that very beautiful song.

Willie continued to work as caretaker of the Carnegie Hall until 1965.

Willie a' Milton loved to watch the cricket matches during the summer and often took the bus to Lerwick to view them on our big television set.

Sylvia Leask presents Willie a' Milton 'Willie Postie' with a wallet of notes on his retirement as postman for the east district of Sandwick. **Photo: Martin Smith**

Having played the game many times while in New Zealand, he knew all the positions, rules etc. On more than one occasion I came home from school to find the front and back doors open, the television on, and grandad fast asleep in the chair 'enjoying' the match. The match had usually been preceded by a visit to the Hayfield Hotel – where his old naval buddy was barman – for a drop of 'Nelson's Blood' (rum) and a yarn!

As a young boy I was fascinated by the tattoos on grandad's hands. He had a small bird on each hand between the thumb and index finger, and a letter on each finger. When the fingers were interlocked they read 'TRUE LOVE'.

A keen gardener, he grew tatties, neeps, lettuce and carrots, winning many prizes at the Cunningsburgh Shows. No doubt the skills he learned at Sandlodge many years before had something to do with this success.

When not watching or 'helping' grandad outside, I used to play with the budgie or the cat inside, and watch him using the leather strop to sharpen his cut-throat razor prior to having a shave. He tested the sharpness of the blade by holding a sheet of newspaper between the thumb and forefinger of his left hand whilst using the razor to cut it from top to bottom without stopping. It always amazed me that he didn't cut himself because he could carry on a conversation whilst he was shaving.

I mentioned earlier that, as a young woman, Chrissie had taken up music. She played the organ in the Sandwick Church of Scotland for over 30 years.

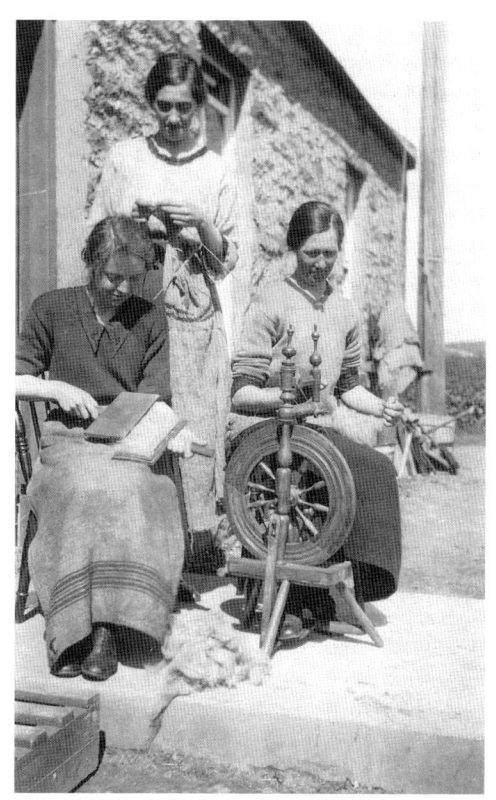

Three ladies carding, knitting and spinning outside the Old Post Office, Stove, Sandwick. Photographer unknown.

She also played the organ for a Sunday school that Miss Wingate held at Sandlodge. In his early years my father would accompany her to the church where he would pump the organ whilst his mother played.

In time the pump organ was replaced with a pedal organ, and some years later with an electric version. Chrissie made the change from one to the other but found it amusing that she could play the electric organ without having to pedal hard with both feet to get enough sound, and could control the volume with the slightest movement of her right foot.

She must have taught well over 100 people to play the organ during her 30-plus years as a private music teacher. Some of her pupils came from Cunningsburgh, travelling to Sandwick on one service bus and catching the return bus home two hours later. Unfortunately, I wasn't sufficiently interested in music at the time and have to admit to being one of her very few failures!

When Chrissie became unwell she moved with Willie to the recently completed Walter and Joan Gray Eventide Home at Scalloway in 1969. Willie a' Milton suffered a stroke there and died in the Gilbert Bain Hospital a few days later, on 28th June, 1970, aged 76.

So ended the life of a man who, like many more of his generation, fought for freedom, King and country, then emigrated to the other side of the world to try and improve their quality of life, and finally did their best for their local community.

Chrissie stayed at Scalloway for a further eight months until she also suffered a stroke and died in the Gilbert Bain Hospital on 9th February, 1971, aged 72.

I spent several months going through her vast collection of music and other material relating to the church and guild that had played such a big part in her life, before distributing it to various churches in Sandwick, Cunningsburgh and Lerwick. Other items, such as the soiree programme for the soldiers, sailors and airmen's return after both world wars, were given to the archives in Lerwick. I think she would have approved.

Grandparents Sand

Adam Ewenson was born at Annfield, Sand, on 12th September, 1890, the youngest of a family of six. Sadly, neither of his two sisters survived into adulthood; the oldest, Anderina, died aged four, and a twin to his brother Andrew was stillborn.

Adam and his three brothers, James, John and Andrew, grew up on the croft. Their father, Andrew senior, was, like many of his generation, a merchant seaman, who was studying to become an officer when an unfortunate accident cut short his career.

Adam and his brothers went to the local school until they were about 14 years of age when they had to leave and find work. Adam became an apprentice to Lerwick builder,

Adam Ewenson (centre) with two fellow sailors. **Photo: A. & A. J. Abernethy, Lerwick**

Adam Ewenson and another during gunnery practice on HMS Vivid.

Jack Irvine, and continued to work for him until, at the age of 24, he was called up to serve King and country in World War One.

Enlisted in the navy, Adam became a leading seaman gunner and served on board the P&O steam ship *Novara* which was being used as a troopship. When the war ended, the money that Adam was due was paid to him in gold sovereigns and half sovereigns.

After the war, Adam returned to work in Lerwick. He was a time-served stonemason and worked on numerous buildings throughout the town including the Town Hall and Quendale House.

He smoked a pipe for most of his life and told me how, on one occasion, he had tried to kick the habit. With others, he was working on the ridge of the Town Hall at the time and left to have his 'holidays' for two weeks during which he didn't smoke at all. When he returned to work he found that his nerve had gone and that he couldn't face the ladders up to the ridge.

When I asked him, "What did you do?" he said, "I had to borrow two cigarettes and smoke them both before I could face the ladders."

After that the pipe was re-instated and he had no more problems.

He also worked on numerous houses; one in Gulberwick that he worked on bears the date of construction in upturned beer bottles just inside the gate.

A house in the country that he was particularly proud of having worked on was the Haa at Reawick where, amongst other things, he installed the water system, using his skills as a stonemason to form the drains in to, and out of, the reservoir.

Building a house at Gulberwick, 1938. From left: Adam Ewenson, mason; Charles Johnson, labourer; Willie Johnson, carpenter; James Smith, mason. Photographer unknown.

It wasn't possible or practical to travel from Sand to Lerwick every day so, like many others, he lodged in Lerwick during the week, travelling home at the weekend either by bus or motorbike, taking with him food and other items not readily available in Sand.

All three of Adam's brothers emigrated from Shetland to the States to take up employment there as miners. One of them, John, later moved to Canada.

Robina Catherine Hunter (Ruby) was born on 18th October, 1896, at Easthouse, South Whiteness, one of a family of nine who, together with their parents, lived in a small traditional Shetland cottage.

She talked about it sometimes and the following two recollections in her own words give some indication of just how difficult life was for her and her brothers and sisters at the time:

> "We used to come home from the school, go and gather whelks, take them to the shop and sell them. We got 9d (4½p) for a bucket full but we got to keep only a penny (½p) for ourselves the rest had to go to buy things for the house like tea and sugar or something to eat for our tea.

> "Sometimes we wir dat hungry we gud oot tae da byre an milked da coo so dat we could get something tae drink afore we gud tae bed."

Ruby was an excellent knitter and used this skill to earn money. She told me how she made socks, gloves and spencers (woollen vests) for sale in Lerwick.

She said:

> "When I had made enough things to sell I would pack them all into a kishie and then set off with my sisters and other women from the district to walk to Lerwick carrying our kishies on our backs. I usually made eleven spencers and laid up number twelve just as we set off. I would finish that one off just as we were coming in the North Road.
>
> "We wore rivlins on our feet because they were better for walking in with the kind of roads we had then. Just outside Lerwick there was a workman's hut, and when we got there we took off our rivlins and put on our shoes for walking round the streets in Lerwick. We left the rivlins in the hut and changed back into them for the walk back home at night."

Having sold their knitting to the buyers in Lerwick they would purchase items for themselves and their homes before setting out on the return journey to South Whiteness, a round trip of some 21 miles.

Ruby started school at the age of six and left when she was 14 years and two months old. She stayed at home helping with the rest of the family until she was 16, when she went to work as a servant to Captain and Mrs Nicholson at Oligarth, Whiteness. Mrs Nicholson had been a matron in various hospitals; her husband a captain on the north boats. Ruby stayed with them for six years.

The Hunter children all went to Sunday School and, when they were older, Ruby and her sister, Eliza, became members of the local church choir. Ruby recalled that the organist, Mrs Isbister, wore very long dresses so they had to be careful not to set their feet on the hem as they walked into the church behind her. She liked Ruby's voice and so always wanted her to stand next to the organ.

Mrs Isbister's husband was a captain, lost with all his crew when their ship sank rounding the horn. Mrs Isbister left instructions that, when she died, she was to be buried at sea.

Grandparents Sand

Ruby Hunter and Adam Ewenson were married by the Reverend L. Scollay, minister at Sand, on 22nd December, 1920, in what is now the Masonic Lodge, Church Road, Lerwick. Their marriage was followed by a reception for their guests in the same venue. Music for the evening was provided by G. Arthur, G Taylor, R. Ganson Jnr, and W. Gray taking turns to play the fiddle; they were accompanied by Miss Anna Sinclair on the piano.

Adam Ewenson and Ruby (nee Hunter) outside Annfield, Sand, late 1950s.
Photo: Martin Smith

Ruby moved in with Adam and his parents at Annfield, Sand. They had three daughters, Helen Rose (Ethel), Robina Adeline Margaret (my mother), and Jean.

They got on well together, Ruby looking after her in-laws as they got older, they in turn looking after the children when they were young and she needed to be doing other things on the croft.

Annfield is about a quarter of a mile from the road and is situated halfway down a steep slope, so going to school wasn't easy for my mother and her two sisters at the best of times, and especially difficult in the winter. I asked Auntie Jean to tell me what it was like. This is what she said:

> "We were in rubber boots the whole winter and when we got to the school our coats, hats and scarves all had to be dried round the big stove in the school ready for us to put on at night when we went home.
>
> "When we were just peerie lasses Santa Claus brought us a new pair of slippers every year; they stayed in the school for us to put on after we took off our rubber boots.
>
> "Mum made up a piece for each one of us every morning which we ate at lunchtime, the teacher made us tea to go with it.
>
> "Mum always had a good meal ready for us when we got home.
>
> "The school opened at 10 am and closed at 4 pm."

(I presume this was so that the children were able to go to school and come home again during the daylight hours in winter.)

Two other stories told to me several times by Granny Ruby and by Auntie Jean, detailed in the book *A Pictorial Daander Trowe Shetland's Crofting Culture*, was how, on one occasion when her mother heard that there was to be a roup (sale) at Sandwater, she set out to walk the 17 miles to the site in order to buy a 'newly calved coo' so that they would have plenty of milk for the family's needs. Having managed to buy the best animal there for £12, she set out to walk the 17 miles back to Annfield, stopping along the way to milk the cow, much to the delight of the people from whom she borrowed the two-gallon pail as they had no cow.

She goes on to recall how their elderly neighbour, who lived on her own and didn't have very much, was left a pail of milk every morning on the fence adjoining their two crofts; the empty pail was collected every night. At the weekend when her father came home with 'sassermaet', two pieces would be delivered to the old lady. Together with the milk and her own vegetables it was probably the most that she had to eat all week. This type of help was common in Shetland and in this case continued until the old lady was no longer able to work the land and left the croft.

There was a shop in Sand, right down at the beach backing on to the churchyard, with living quarters above. A small pier next to the shop was used to land the goods from the boat (thought to have been called *The Ark*) that arrived on a regular basis from Scalloway.

When younger and fitter and the family was growing up, trips were often made by boat across Sandsound Voe to the shop on the other side. My mother talked of having done this many times. On occasions when her father was in Lerwick and maybe couldn't get home in the wintertime because the roads were blocked, she would go with her mother or her sisters to get essential supplies from the Sandsound shop on the other side of the voe.

Other people from the district used the crossing point at Annfield to get to the Sandsound shop. On arrival at Annfield they would lay a sign (usually a piece of white cloth) on the peat stacks at the top of the banks. The men in the shop would see this and row over to fetch them, putting them back across when they had got all their messages which then had to be carried home.

Grandparents and great-grandparents before her made the same journey to Da Store situated down at the shore just a little further north. Mother could remember Da Store and the house being flooded on several occasions during bad weather and high tides, although it wasn't being used as a shop when she was young.

As roads and vehicles improved, several grocery vans visited the area every week bringing much-needed supplies. Although the Ewensons had their own potatoes, hens, eggs (preserved in a substance called Water Glass, available from Gansons in 1lb or 2lb tins), vegetables, a cow, and some sheep, during the years when the family was growing up, the visiting vans were a lifeline in later years.

In the spring of the year, Adam would cast the family peat banks at the point of Saltness, near the Mill Burn, and these would then be raised and turned by Ruby. When my mother and her sisters were very young their grandparents looked after them whilst their mother went to the peat hill.

When they were older they helped with the peats and the grandparents would look after the house and have a meal ready for them when they returned.

The point of Saltness is at least a mile from Annfield and the only way to get there to work the peats was to walk along the cliff top. Having got there, Ruby had to work all day, shelter from any rain, and then walk back home. It could not have been easy for her, particularly when the family was young.

When Adam came home for his 'holidays' he would take his boat (the fourareen *Baabie*), initially rigged with fore and aft sails, and 'flit' the peats home to the noost at Annfield. The larger peats were thrown loose into the boat so that they could get more in and only when the boat had been well loaded in this way did they put bags of peats on top. Ruby worked the jib sheet whilst Adam looked after the main and steered the heavily laden boat.

On arrival at the noost the peats then had to be unloaded from the boat by hand and barrowed above the 'banks', where one or more stacks were built to prevent them from being taken away by the sea. The peats were then taken up the steep slope to the house. For many years this was done using a horse and cart. All this work meant that the peats had to be handled several times, a truly back-breaking task.

Adam Ewenson (left) and John Isbister load bags of peats into Adam's boat for the trip to the noost at Annfield, Sand. **Photo: Jean Isbister**

Grandparents Sand

Above: Underway –heading down Tresta Voe to Annfield. Adam Ewenson is aft operating the Anzani outboard. John Isbister is forward. Note space left so that oars could be used if the engine failed.

Below: Adam Ewenson (left) and John Isbister taking the bags of peats from the noost up above the 'banks' at Annfield. **Photos: Jean Isbister**

Adam Ewenson taking his peats up to Annfield, three bags at a time, on his motorbike. **Photo: John Isbister**

In 1947, Adam acquired two Anzani outboard motors with long shafts and used these instead of the sails. Only one was used to actually power the boat; the other was carried in case of a breakdown. This was much quicker, safer and less weather-dependent, so the flitting could be done at times when it would not have been possible using the sails. It also meant that more and faster trips could be made to and from the point of Saltness, so almost all the peats could be bagged before they were loaded into the boat.

Adam, like many men of his time, was a resourceful man; he made and fitted to his Raleigh motorbike a wooden pannier structure capable of taking three bags of peats at a time. Using this system the peats were taken straight from the top of the banks up to the house. This reduced the number of times the peats had to be handled and saved a considerable amount of time and effort. He continued to use this method for many years.

(Note: James Ewenson, Adam's grandfather, died of a heart attack in his boat on the way home from working his peats on 19th June, 1878.)

In 1967, Adam suffered a stroke which robbed him of the ability to swallow or speak. After a spell in hospital and some time spent with his daughter Jean and her husband John in Yell, he returned to Annfield to be looked after by Ruby, who had just had her sight restored following a successful cataract operation.

For the next 18 months, Ruby looked after Adam, feeding him through a nasal gastric tube. No mean feat for a woman in her late-70s who didn't have a telephone; and there was no road to their croft. If she needed medical help she had to leave Adam and go to their neighbour's house and get John Smith to walk approximately a mile to the telephone box to phone for the doctor.

Adam died on 3rd April, 1969, aged 78. That night the undertakers came to Annfield carrying the coffin on their shoulders, wrapped loosely in a black velvet cloth, the brass handles flashing in the sunlight as the cloth flapped about in the wind. My cousin Ronnie and I watched as the undertakers completed their task before letting the family pay their last respects. That done, Adam's coffin was taken outside and placed on trestles. Six of us took a brass handle each and, at a signal from the undertaker, lifted the coffin, and proceeded to carry it out over the hill to the hearse waiting at the roadside. The undertakers followed alongside carrying the trestles. We stopped several times, resting the coffin on the trestles and changed sides so that we weren't always lifting with the same hand. On arrival at the main road the coffin was placed in the hearse and taken to the church, where it remained until the funeral next day.

Ruby stayed in Annfield for a number of years after Adam's death. I always thought that it had to be a very lonely existence and so one night said to her, "Granny, is it no awful lonely sitting here in Annfield all on your own?"

"Sit down and I'll tell you about loneliness," she said. "I sit here in the chair night after night just alone with my thoughts. Every night about eight o'clock a spider comes out from behind the range, runs across my feet to the edge of the mat, then it runs off across the floor and up behind the china cabinet. After about an hour it runs back across the floor, across my feet, and back in behind the range. I think it must be finding something to eat at the back of the cabinet."

I have recalled that story many times and still can't imagine just how long you have to sit still on your own and watch that spider before you realise that it is a regular occurrence and look forward to it happening again and again. I have never heard a better description of loneliness.

In 1975, Ruby moved to the sheltered houses at Weisdale. She enjoyed her time there because there was so much going on around her and people of a similar age and background to talk to and visit.

In her 91st year, Ruby suffered a broken hip and, after several weeks in hospital in Lerwick, died of the complications and shock brought on by such an event, on 20th January, 1988. She was laid to rest next to her beloved Adam in the Sand churchyard.

Coming Together

Adeline Ewenson holding Averil Tait, Sandwick, 1940. Photographer unknown.

Robina Adeline Margaret Ewenson left school in 1937, at the age of 14, and went to work as a servant to Maggie Johnson (known as Maggie o' Tulkie) who lived in Sand. She was with her until 1939 when she moved to the Church of Scotland Manse, also in Sand. In March, 1940, she got a job as a nanny to Alec and Mary Tait who had a furniture business at 3 Market Street in Lerwick.

Alec Tait also had a haulage business and had secured a contract to run men and materials to Sumburgh where various kinds of air raid shelters and other wartime constructions were being put up. In order for him to be nearer to his work, the family moved to Sandwick in August, 1940. Adeline moved with them to Central Cottage, Sandwick.

It was while she was living and working in Sandwick that Adeline decided to take music lessons from

Chrissie Smith, who lived just down the road from Central Cottage at Victoria Cottage, and it was there that she met Willie Smith. He had left school in 1935 and gone to work in Halcrows' shop at Stove, Sandwick. From there he moved to Thomson's where he drove various vehicles including heavy trucks until he was called up for service in World War Two and joined the Royal Air Force.

Willie Smith, the author's father, taken outside Halcrow's shop at Sandwick, sometime between 1937 and 1940. Photographer unknown.

During the war years young servicemen didn't have much money with which to buy their wives or girlfriends gifts or tokens of affection so they had to improvise. Willie and his RAF friends specialised in several items that made use of the RAF wings and crown. For example, they cut a heart shape from a piece of Perspex (an early form of plastic), filed and polished the edges and then, having carefully cut the RAF wings and crown from buttons etc. placed them on the Perspex and applied heat with a soldering iron to imbed them. A neck chain was then added.

Another item of jewellery that Willie made for both his girlfriend and her sister was a wrist bangle in the form of a snake. To do this a thin strip was cut from the sheet of Perspex and the edges filed and sandpapered with ever-finer sheets of water emery paper until they were smooth. A mug was then filled with hot water and the 'snake' inserted to soften the Perspex which was then wound round and round the inside of the mug. This took some time and wasn't easy on the hands because the hot water had to be topped up when it started to cool, until the 'snake' had been wound round the mug three times. Two small pieces of red Perspex or glass were then inserted in the head end, again using heat from a small soldering iron. The finished snake was then given a final polish with Duraglit.

Tie pins in the shape of aircraft were fashioned out of thin copper sheet; and cigarette lighters made using two half-penny coins and a piece of copper pipe. One half-penny was soldered on to each side of a piece of copper pipe about an inch wide. Two holes a short distance apart were drilled in the main copper pipe and smaller pieces inserted, one with a cover to hold the wick which passed into the main body of the lighter, the other the flint wheel, flint and spring. Cotton wool was then inserted into the middle piece of copper pipe via the flint wheel aperture; this held the petrol and transferred it to the wick. A considerable amount of work went into getting all the joints tight so that the petrol didn't escape. The finished lighter was then polished.

These hand-made gifts were treasured by the recipients and went on to become lifetime reminders of the difficult times the couples experienced when their lives together were just beginning.

In 1943, the Gilbert Bain Hospital was looking for domestic staff and, as her sister Jean Ewenson was now living and working in Lerwick, Adeline applied for and got a job there. After a few months she started training to be a nurse.

However, things were about to go badly wrong. A Norwegian seaman was brought into the Gilbert Bain with what turned out to be the common measles. This is a very serious disease even today, but in 1943 complications and even death was common. Several members of the domestic and nursing staff, including Adeline, contacted the measles. She was very ill, developing the complications of double pneumonia and a mastoid in her right ear. Thankfully, she survived the pneumonia so surgeon Daniel Lamont was able to operate on her ear. Unfortunately, the operation wasn't a success and she lost her hearing on that side.

At the time that Adeline was lying seriously ill in the isolation hospital, Willie Smith was based at RAF Swinderby. Enlisted in the motor transport section of the RAF, Willie drove all kinds of vehicles associated with the work of a busy airfield including fuel tankers, ambulances, cranes, and large trucks designed to carry bombs to the aircraft. These included Vickers Wellingtons, Avro Manchesters and the famous Avro Lancasters.

He described how, when instructed to take men out to the practice bombing ranges, it was possible to count the ribs of the fuselage through the open bomb bay doors as the aircraft flew low overhead. Small incendiary bombs were dropped and the resulting small fires told the aircrew how close they were to the targets. It was the job of the ground staff to put out these fires before they got out of control.

Another job was of course to transport bombs to the aircraft. One cold and very frosty winter morning Willie's truck was stopped at the top of the hill above the airfield by a civilian policeman who wanted to check what he was carrying. On seeing the bombs, he said, "You're not going down that steep icy road with those, are you?"

Willie's mate replied, "Yes, of course we are, unless you know of another route."

On hearing this and having seen the number of bombs on the truck the policeman told them to give him two minutes, got on his bike and pedalled like hell in the opposite direction! The transport crew in the next truck couldn't understand why there was no policeman on duty when they arrived at the same checkpoint. They found the answer when they caught up with Willie and his mate at the airfield, where they all had a good laugh about it.

Of course, there were far more serious events that took place on an airfield operated by bomber command. At night trucks with several men in each would be sent to various locations and at a given time, and no doubt depending on the prevailing weather conditions, the men would be instructed to turn on the runway lights at their particular location for a specified number of minutes. The men knew how many planes had gone out on a raid so they were able to count the number returning – the numbers weren't always the same.

Willie said that the hardest job of all was removing the dead and injured from the aircraft. In many cases they knew the men involved, and had spoken to them or driven them out to the aircraft just a few hours earlier. He made the comment that "the life expectancy of a rear gunner was seven weeks." It's no wonder that he only ever spoke about his experiences at RAF Swinderby on a very few occasions.

Whilst he was involved in the daily routine of the airfield, he also had the added worry of knowing that his girlfriend of two years was lying seriously ill in the isolation hospital in Lerwick. Naturally, he was very concerned about her and no one could tell him whether she would survive her illness or not. I don't know if they had discussed getting married or not, but he bought an engagement ring and posted it to her.

Thankfully, she survived her ordeal and, for all I know, receiving an engagement ring in those circumstances might just have been the encouragement that she needed to fight for her life and a future with her boyfriend, Willie.

After a period of recovery at home in Annfield, and knowing that having lost her hearing she could not pass a medical and would never be called up for war service, Adeline went to work for Doctor Morrison at Parkhall, Bixter.

Doctor Morrison had two sons. One of them would often go out on to the flat roof and walk up and down playing the bagpipes. Sometimes they would both go out shooting and bring back snipe and other birds for Adeline and the cook to clean and prepare for dinner.

Parkhall had its own water supply but because the storage tank was below the level of the house the water had to be pumped up. A small petrol engine was used for this purpose and Adeline had to learn how to operate it along with all her other duties, which sometimes included helping the doctor to mix up cough medicine and dispense tablets!

She enjoyed her time at Parkhall and in later years could hardly bare to look at it in its dilapidated state.

Adeline Ewenson and Willie Smith were married by the Rev. George Smith on 27th April, 1945, in the U.F. Manse, South Road, Lerwick, now called Breiwick House. After the ceremony they went to Scalloway to have their photographs taken by Clement Williamson, and then on to their reception in the Sand School (I have been told that theirs was the last wedding reception to be held in the Sand School).

During the war years everything was rationed so you had to make do with what you could get, and improvise. Their wedding cake only had marzipan and icing on the top, stiff white card was put round the outside

Coming Together 41

Above: Best man Stanley 'Milton' Sothcott, groom Willie Smith, bride Adeline Ewenson, bridesmaid Jean Ewenson, 27th April, 1945. Reproduced by permission of W. Smith, Scalloway.
Photo: C. J. Williamson

Right: Adeline Smith (née Ewenson) studio photo taken after her marriage to Willie Smith. **Photo: R. H. Ramsay**

to make it look as if the cake was iced all round. Beer was in short supply but somehow or other they managed to get a barrel from somewhere.

Willie had been posted 'overseas' to Sullom Voe, so after their marriage they moved into lodgings at Brae with Maggie Tulloch. Adeline got a job working in the Church of Scotland canteen at Sullom Voe.

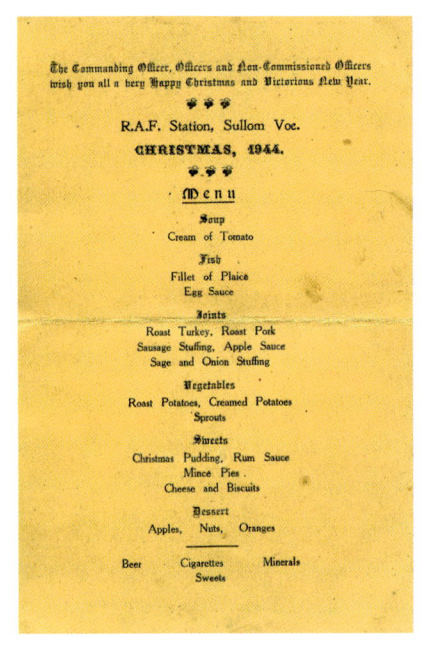

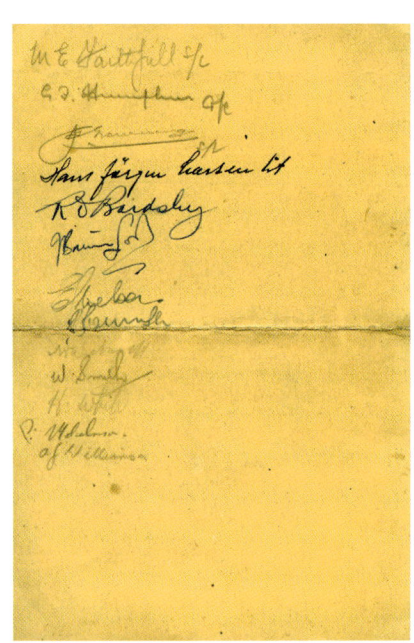

RAF Sullom Voe Christmas 1944 menu with signatures on reverse.

Sullom Voe was an important base for various types of flying boats and both Adeline and Willie had many stories to tell about the aircraft and the crews who flew in them. They were never allowed to fly in the aircraft of course, but both were on board them at various times, ashore and afloat.

All went well for the newly married couple until, in November, 1945, one week after the war finished, Willie was posted to India!

The following is his account of the voyage from Liverpool to Bombay:

> 9th Dec 1945 Sunday – Boarded the Empress of Australia at Liverpool – Sleeping in hammocks.
> 10th Dec – Foggy morning. Sailed about two o'clock. Canteen opened.
> 11th Dec – Lovely trip all day. Saw a few small ships.
> 12th Dec – In the Bay now, pretty rough, saw an aircraft-carrier and a schooner.
> 13th Dec – Passed Cape St. Vincent this morning, and expect to be passing Gibraltar tonight 2100. Lovely weather.

14th Dec – In the Med now, lovely weather, passing Algiers later tonight.
15th Dec – Passed some small islands and ships pretty hot weather now. Clocks 1 hour forward.
16th Dec – Passed Sicily early morning.
17th Dec – Posted our mail, should be at Port Said tomorrow.
18th Dec – Arrived P. Said 9 o' Clock lovely place plenty of things to buy. Left at 10 o' clock.
19th Dec – Well through the Suez now two ships following us. Saw natives, camels scrap etc.
20th Dec – Well in through the Red Sea now, getting very hot changed into Khaki Dress.
21st Dec – Sea a bit rough now, but weather is still hot, posted mail again.
22nd Dec – Lovely day again saw a few small islands tonight. Sleeping on deck 98 degrees below decks!
23rd Dec – Arrived at Aden early this morning watching the natives fight for pennies.
24th Dec – Was at a concert this afternoon. Dancing and carol singing on deck tonight, hot weather.
25th Dec – Not much of a Xmas, but the dinner wasn't bad. I think this is the first day we haven't seen a ship or a bit of land.
26th Dec – Weather is rainy and colder now, saw some flying-fish, boxing on deck in the afternoon. Changed money.
27th Dec – I had a tooth out today on board the ship, we arrived in Bombay about four o' clock this afternoon, but we won't be going off the ship till tomorrow.
28th Dec – Disembarked at Bombay, went to transit camp about four miles outside. One letter from home.
29th Dec – Some more letters from home, got paid 40 rupees today. (about £2)
30th Dec – Day off today, got photos taken. Met two Shetland boys.
31st Dec – Going to Bombay with the boys tonight.

Willie was in the motor transport section of the Royal Air Force and spent the next few months driving all kinds of trucks, cranes etc., moving equipment that had been sent out to India in preparation for the Far East Campaign back to the docks for shipment back to Britain.

44   Hoswick Man

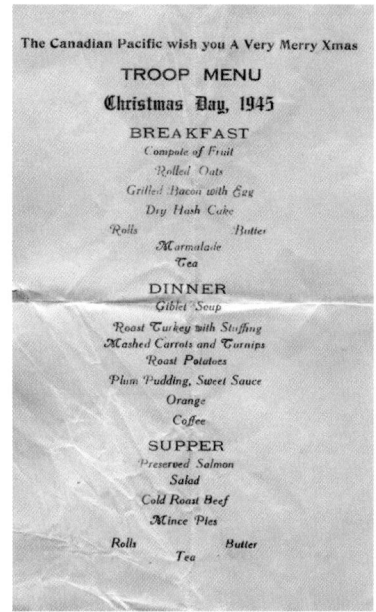

Above left: 1693183 Cpl. Smith W., RAF.

Above right: Troop menu.

Below: The Taj Mahal photographed by Willie Smith in 1946.

Above: Willie Smith and others at a milestone in India, 1946.

Right: Willie Smith and others, India, 1946.

Amongst the many items they transported were hundreds of aircraft that had been sent out in crates to be assembled out there, or used as spare parts. He talked of seeing football pitches with nothing on them but fridges for the officers' quarters and camp beds piled 20 high standing in rows.

I found the following poem amongst his wartime papers:

Lanka Lament

They call it the Garden of Eden
A gem in a sun-kissed sea
Far famed for its fruit and flowers
And wonderful nectar like tea

They forgot the savage mosquitoes
The blood-thirsty dive-bombing sods
That poison your blood with diseases
In this garden the playground of gods

They forgot the other little insects
The ant with its razor like fang
The rats, the bats, the beetles
And the rest of the murderous gang

They forgot to mention the heat-rash
And the nights when you swelter and sweat
In the oven like heat that enfolds you
In the power that you can never forget

They forgot the drums that awake you
At intervals during the night
The chanting, the wailing, the howling
In which natives and canines delight

They forgot just where they have put us
Far far away from all fun
From cinemas, cafes and canteens
Is there no escape from this sun?

And what about all the diseases
Like elephantitis and gleet
Malaria, dysentery, sunstroke
And hook-worms that gnaw at your feet

COMING TOGETHER 47

*They call it the Garden of Eden
A gem in a sun-kissed sea
But if this is the Garden of Eden
The back-yard at home will do me*

Written in my father's hand but the author is unknown.

On the day that the troop ship he was on left Bombay, a message came over the Tannoy to the effect that it was not necessary to keep their kit! Hundreds of rifles, steel helmets, gas masks, webbing etc. were immediately thrown overboard into Bombay harbour, amidst loud cheers and much excitement. The journey back to Britain took three weeks, bringing to an end Willie's four years and three months war service.

Willie took several souvenirs home with him from India. These included watches for his wife and his sister-in-law, an ivory necklace of carved elephants, and a small highly polished chromium box with a picture of the SS *Empress of Australia* on the lid. Behind the picture is a beautiful sea and sky and it is only when you look closer that you discover they are actually made from a butterfly's wings.

Above: Improvised birthday card. No fancy cards or time to shop for one during the war years.

Right: Willie Smith with one of the trucks he drove in India in 1946. Note the air conditioning.

ABOARD THE R.M.S. "STRATHNAVER"
IN THE
SUEZ CANAL

"SOUVENIR CARD"

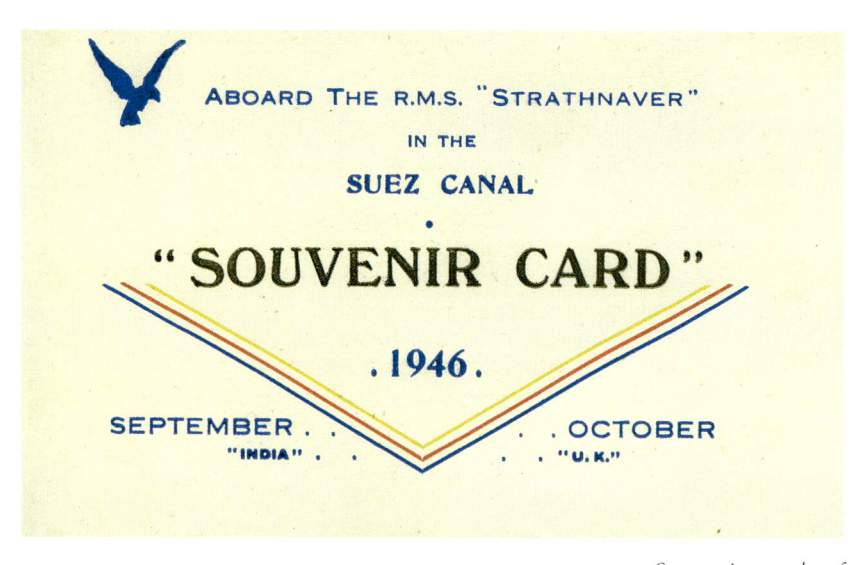

.1946.

SEPTEMBER . . . . . OCTOBER
"INDIA" . . . . "U.K."

Specifications

Tonnage: Gross 22282.75
Speeds: Full 18.5 knots.
Average 17 knots.

Builders: Vickers Armstrong, Barrow.

Engines: B.T.H., Rugby.
B.H.P. 28000

Length O.A. 664 ft. 2 ins.   Breadth 80 ft. 2 ins.
Height of Mast 152 ft.   Height of Funnel 102 ft.
from l.w.l.   from l.w.l.

Souvenir card of the troopship that Willie Smith came home on from India, 1946.

On his return to Shetland in 1946, Willie and Adeline moved into the rear flat of Thomson's Buildings in Hoswick (now called the Orca Country Inn, formerly the Barclay Arms). They moved to Garden Cottage in November, 1947, to prepare for the birth of their first child.

I was delivered into this world by caesarean section on the morning of Friday, 21st May, 1948, by Mr Daniel Lamont, surgeon at the Gilbert Bain Hospital; Doctor Mackenzie and Sister Walker assisted.

The first month of my life was spent with my grandparents and great-grandmother in Rocklea, Stove, whilst my mother recovered from the surgery. In 1948, a 'section' involved an incision some 25cm long. This, together with the anaesthetic chloroform, made recovery long and difficult, my mother being unable to lift anything, including me, for several months.

At what should have been a very happy time for my mother and father there was the added burden of how they were going to pay for my birth. The National Health Service still did not exist so the cost of Mr Lamont and others had to be paid by them.

Garden Cottage, Hoswick, 1948/49. Young man on bicycle unknown. Note the size of the 'lean-to'. **Photo: Willie Smith**

The total charge for bringing me into the world was £100 (£2,720 in 2008). Raising that amount when the average weekly wage was just £5 to £8 per week must have been a great strain on top of everything else.

Seventeen days after I was born my mother took the bus to Lerwick to register my birth. My father couldn't take time off because he needed to earn as much as possible to help pay the hospital bill, and all the other things that a new baby needs, in addition to their normal living expenses. No maternity leave in 1948!

When my mother was well enough we all moved back to Garden Cottage in Hoswick. It was there that I was to spend the next 14 years of my life.

Garden Cottage was constructed in the traditional Shetland style with a 'but' and 'ben' and a 'closet'. The partitions were all wooden 'v'-lining; in addition there was a wooden 'lean-to' and an outside toilet. There was no public sewage system or water supply in Hoswick at the time so all the water for cooking, cleaning and washing had to be carried from the communal well, 100 yards away.

When I was about 18 months old the 'lean-to' became the subject of a dispute between our neighbour, old Bonnar, and the owner of the cottage. Old Bonnar said that the 'lean-to' had been built some six feet in

Garden Cottage, Hoswick, Sandwick, mid-1950s. **Photo: Willie Smith**

COMING TOGETHER 51

Above: The Hoswick well, sadly not as well cared for today as it was in the 1950s.

Below: This house, next to the Hoswick well, was the birthplace of Malcolm Smith, later Sir Malcolm Smith, of Malcolm Smith Trawlers Ltd.   ***Photos: Martin Smith***

over his property, the owner of the cottage disagreed. The laird was called to settle the dispute and old Bonnar was proved right. So the crosscut saw was laid on and the 'lean-to' reduced in width by some six feet.

We were left with a 'lean-to' about four feet wide, just big enough to serve as a small kitchen with a stove and storage cupboards. In this area the cooking and laundry, including washing all my nappies, was done by hand. There was no insulation in the walls or roof so the stove had to be kept lit for as long as possible to stop the cold air from getting into the main house, and to enable clothes to be dried inside when the weather was bad.

Nurse Minnie Tulloch visited regularly to attend to my mother and keep an eye on my progress. Just three

Top left: *Martin Smith (the author) in the garden at Garden Cottage. Note part of the 'lean-to' is missing; this was removed after an argument between the house owner and the neighbour.*

Left: *Minnie Tulloch holding Martin Smith (the author), 1950/51.* **Photos: Willie Smith**

years after a world war many items were still rationed or in very short supply. Orange juice came in bottles in concentrated form, baby milk in cardboard drums with strict instructions as to how it was to be made up, and how often baby was to be fed. The allocated amount had to last until the nurse came again.

Despite these problems I grew up just like any other child of the time and was no doubt spoilt by my parents, grandparents at Sand and Sandwick, and my great-grandmother at Rocklea.

Four generations of the Smith family. From left: Andrina Smith, Chrissie Smith, Martin Smith, Adeline Smith (Ewenson), Willie Smith.

Making Ends Meet

For a small community of just over 40 houses, Hoswick had a wide variety of employment. Crofting was of course the main source of income and was often supplemented by other employment, for example, as weavers and knitters to L. J. Smith. L. J. Smith's shop and weaving sheds employed several people from Hoswick and Sandwick as well as numerous hand and machine knitters from all over Sandwick, Levenwick, Cunningsburgh and the Ness.

One crofter, Bertie Nicolson, diversified into what was known as 'deep litter hens' – a forerunner of the caged method of keeping hens. He told me that he used this method from 1951 until 1961 when the price of feed went up and the price of eggs came down. Another man, F. W. Cocker, started a pig farm. I can remember being taken to see a sow and piglets on more than one occasion.

Some of the buildings used for storage were made from fishing boat hulls, possibly even ones that had operated out of Broonies Taing. One or two crofts were still using horses for some of their work up until the mid- to late-1950s. They were replaced by their mechanical equivalents – the Iron Horse and the Massey Ferguson tractor.

Tractors are dangerous things. One local man had a narrow escape when the plough he was using jammed under a rock. He put on the foot brake and got off to see what could be done to free it. Whilst he was doing this a sudden jolt caused the brake to jump off and the tractor set off down the steep hill and finished up on the rocks below.

Cockers pigs at Hoswick. Note the use of old fishing boat hulls for storage, etc. These may have fished from Broonies Taing at one time. **Photo: Willie Smith**

Some farmers shot rabbits and sold their skins, for which they were paid 12/- (60p) per dozen. If they shot an otter the skin could fetch 55/- (£2 15s) which, at the time, would have been almost half a week's wages. No wonder the poor animals were hunted to near extinction.

Several men were carpenters or joiners and either worked from home or were employed by local contractors. Lowrie Nicolson was a carpenter and also the local undertaker.

Jimmy Sinclair had a truck and two cars for hire. I spent many an enjoyable night in his garage giving him a hand to change the layout of the truck from carrying livestock to peats etc. Like most small boys with an interest in all things mechanical, I knew where every bolt and nut had to go.

One or two men were still going to the whaling in the early '50s. There was always great excitement when they came back home and showed you a whale's eardrum or a sperm whale's tooth. They had many wonderful stories to tell and fascinating photographs to show of huge whales tied alongside the factory ships, seals, and brightly coloured penguins. Some of the scrimshaw work that they brought home was just amazing.

Then there were the bakers and shop assistants employed by the Sandwick Baking Company and George R. Jamieson's; the butchers in Peter Barclay's meat shop at the Central; and the shop assistants at Halcrow's shop at Stove.

Christie Johnson and John Barclay had their own shoe shops and, in addition to selling footwear, they provided the full cobblers' service. Mr W. J. Smith (Billy) had a photographer's shop at Central, Sandwick. The name was changed to Stove & Smith when he was joined by Mr T. W. Stove (Tom). Both men took pictures of weddings and other events throughout Shetland for a number of years. I can recall going to the shop with my father to pick up prints and see if the pictures that I had taken had come out correctly or not.

The solitary petrol pump at Stove was operated by Margaret Goudie, a sister to Magnus Goudie, the bus driver. During a recent conversation she told me that it took 28 turns of the handle to fill the glass tank on the pump with a gallon of petrol. Then she had to check that there wasn't any water or debris in the petrol before opening the valve to let it run into the vehicle. The valve was then closed and the process repeated until the vehicle was full, or the customer had got what he wanted. That meant that when her brother came with the bus for 20 gallons of fuel, Margaret had to turn the pump handle 560 times!

Then there were the grocery van men, like my father and Andrew Duncan, and later on the mobile butcher's van owned and operated by Magnie Geordie Smith.

Several women were employed in the school canteen, and at least two male janitors to look after the heating systems and carry out any necessary repairs and maintenance.

Some men went to the drift net fishing in the summer and found other jobs for the rest of the year; others worked on the roads.

In the early '50s, a public water scheme was started for the whole of Sandwick and my father and several others worked on that scheme for some months. He told me that there were places in the hill where the diggers couldn't work because the ground was soft so they all got tuskars and cast out the pipe track.

Several men made 'claws' or wrecking bars from off-cuts of the steel reinforcing rods used in the dam supplying the water to the filter system. I recently gave my father's one to the men in the LHD wire store, who will make more use of it than I ever could.

Prior to my birth and during my early years mother supplemented father's wages by hand-knitting gloves and jumpers for the Shetland

Hand Knitters Association. The finished articles were sent to Lerwick by Thomson's bus; payment was made by post a few days later in the form of postal orders.

The following is a sample of the prices paid to her at the time:

> 12th October 1947 for 6 pairs of Ladies Gloves @ 14/- (70p) £4.20
> 23rd Dec. 1947 for 6 pairs of Fair Isle Gloves @ 8/3d (41½) £2.49
> 8th January 1948 for 5 pairs Ladies Gloves @ 14/- (70p) £3.50
> 23rd Sept. 1950 for 1 Fair Isle Border Cardigan 22 inches £1.05

There was a huge demand for Shetland knitwear at the time with buyers from as far away as London advertising for supplies. In *The Shetland Times* of 24th September, 1948, L. J. Smith, Hoswick, placed an advert for the following:

> 5,000 pairs of Ladies Fair Isle Gloves
> 2,000 pairs of Children's Fair Isle Gloves
> Also Berets, Fair Isle Jumpers, Short Sleeve All / Over Jumpers and Lace Pullovers.

In the late 1950s, my mother purchased a Rapidex 160 knitting machine for £28 19s 6d (£28.97½) and was taught how to make jumpers on it by Andrew Mullay from Bigton. She chose this machine because there wasn't much room in our house and the Rapidex was small and neat whilst still able to do a good job.

Wool was made up in hanks that had to be transferred on to cones that fitted on to the rear of the Rapidex before any knitting could start. This was done using the 'yarn winders' that came with the machine. You placed the hank of wool

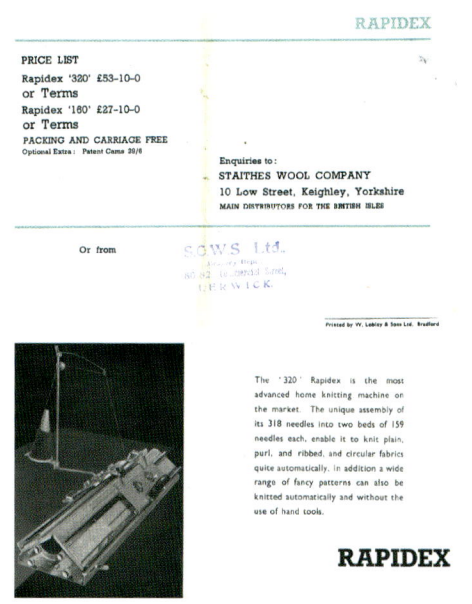

Rapidex knitting machine of the type used by Adeline Smith in the 1950/60s.

in the expanding arms of the unit, put a cone on the winder and cranked the handle with one hand whilst holding a large block of wax in the other making sure that the wool ran over it. The waxed wool slid more easily round the various parts of the Rapidex and into the needles.

Yarn winding took up a lot of time if you had a large order to fulfil so quite often I did this so that my mother could get on with the knitting part of the operation. I know several other boys and girls of my age who did the same.

The machine itself came with a series of steel weights that were supplemented with home-made ones made of lead. These were used whenever thick or heavy wool jumpers were being made, to pull the garment down from the knitting beds. God help you if you got up speed and the wool broke, for the whole lot fell at your feet!

From time to time I would work the machine so that my mother could get on with something else, or just have a well earned rest. If she was working on a plain sleeve or body all I had to do was carefully push the knitting unit backwards and forwards until the counter told me that I had reached the right number of rows. The clever part was in the skill needed to get the tension right throughout the whole garment, knit in the fair isle yoke and then, using a bodkin needle, 'graft' the various parts together properly to complete the jumper. That done the jumper had to be 'dressed' on a jumper board, and then folded neatly for the buyer.

Most of my mother's machine knitting was sold to Willie Johnson who had a shop in Reform Lane, in Lerwick.

My mother, and hundreds like her, spent many long hours slaving over their knitting machines trying to make ends meet. Some men and women even turned it into a full time occupation, building sheds to hold the machines and employing women to knit in the Fair Isle and then 'graft' together the various parts of the jumpers. In this way they could make a lot more jumpers and women who didn't have, didn't want, or perhaps couldn't afford a knitting machine, could make some money putting in the Fair Isle yokes, grafting and finishing the jumpers.

One way or another, knitting machines helped to improve the lives of many Shetland families, even if it was only in a small way.

Entertainments and Hobbies

In the early 1950s, every house had a wireless set powered by a 'wet battery' or accumulator. The accumulator stood about nine inches high, was made of glass and contained several glass tubes as well as distilled water and acid. This meant that it was fairly heavy, so it usually stood either on the floor underneath the set, or on a shelf or a table alongside it. Two copper wires ran from the accumulator to connections at the rear of the set and a further two came from the set to a large copper switch, usually mounted somewhere close to the window where the aerial and the earth wires came into and went out from the house.

Outside you had to have a 'long wire' aerial mounted as high up as possible, with insulators at either end and at the point of entry into the house. The length of wire was important as this tuned the aerial to the range of frequencies that you wanted to listen to.

The earth wire was equally important and should ideally terminate with a good piece of copper pipe or plate buried in the ground.

The two-position switch was then used to select either the aerial position when you wanted to listen to the radio, or the earth position when the wireless was switched off.

It was important when not using the radio set to remember to leave the switch in the earth position, so that in the event of lightning striking the long wire aerial outside, the extremely high voltage surge would travel along the aerial wire through the switch and directly to earth.

One local man forgot to do this before he went to Lerwick and came back to find that lightning had struck his long wire aerial, travelled along it and, being unable to run to earth, had blown a hole in his house window causing the stonework to collapse. Perhaps it was fortunate that he was out of the house at the time.

The wireless set, as it came to be known, was used daily to listen to the news, weather forecasts, and by a lot of men to what was known as the trawler wave band, to hear how the fishing boats were getting on. At 9pm, the north boats – *St Clair*, *St Magnus* and *St Rognvald* – exchanged details of their positions and the weather conditions as they made their way to and from Aberdeen and Lerwick. This gave listeners information about the weather and whether or not the boats would arrive in Lerwick and Aberdeen on time.

When the accumulator lost its charge it had to be taken to someone who had the necessary equipment to recharge it or refill it with distilled water and acid. In Sandwick this was John Williamson who, in addition to recharging or refilling the accumulators, also mended clocks and watches.

As young boys we used to visit him from time to time seeking the glass tubes from inside the accumulators; these were to be used as peashooters. Sometimes John hadn't had time to wash the tubes thoroughly and he would warn us to do so before we used them. If we didn't we could taste the acid on our lips and tongue.

Having got your peashooter the next stop was to one of the local shops for ammunition – a small packet of barley.

Sandwick Concert Party. From left – back: Tom Jamieson, Jim Jamieson, John Jamieson, Jack Bray, Tom Leslie, Jackie Pottinger. Front: Maureen Jamieson, Greta Jamieson, Myra Youngclause, Wilma Duncan, Janette Halcrow, Jessamine Leisk, Valmai Barclay, Christyne Munro, Elspeth Jamieson, Annabell Bray. At the piano is Christabelle Jamieson. **Photo: T. W. Stove**

My father had a keen interest in all things mechanical and electrical, so when he had saved up enough money he bought a Collaro turntable. This he installed in an old radio cabinet which had a lid that lifted up. The turntable had a 'line-out' facility so that the music could be played through the amplifier of the radio using the 'line-in' facility.

Over time my parents collected a number of '78' records, most of which I still have and will convert into the latest digital format just in case the originals get broken.

Just two houses away from Garden Cottage lived the Harper boys – Jimmy, John and Billy. Billy was a merchant seaman so I didn't really see him very much. John and Jimmy had all manner of things that we, as small boys, used to enjoy, amongst them a movie projector which they used to show us cartoons.

On one occasion we were all enjoying the film when someone noticed that one of the old men was missing. The room light was switched on and it was discovered that he had slipped off his chair and disappeared under the table. A closer look revealed that he had had too much 'home brew' to drink. His breathing seemed okay, so they put the light out again and resumed the programme of cartoons!

You could always tell when someone in the village was going to make a 'brew' because they washed out all the bottles at the communal well, leaving a lovely smell that lasted for days!

John Harper, like my father, had acquired a gramophone and a much bigger and more powerful amplifier. On fine summer days he would open the two upstairs skylights and put a loudspeaker in each one, facing outwards. The whole village was then treated to the latest records, sometimes for hours at a time.

John and Jimmy also had motorbikes which were of great interest to us young boys; we loved looking at all the different types of bike and sitting on them. Occasionally John or Jimmy would take us for short runs to the Central Shop or up to the Sooth Ness and back, which was a great thrill. At the weekends a number of their friends would come to Hoswick to check out each other's latest machines and no doubt some of the lovely young women who lived in the village at the time.

As a result of all this activity, Hoswick was a very busy place at the weekends with lots of noise and the sound of happy young voices. Sadly, all this came to a very sad end when, on the evening of 29th June, 1960, John Harper, aged 22, and his best friend Jim Jamieson, aged just 18, were killed in an accident at Fladdabister. From then on the weekends in Hoswick were eerily silent.

My father's love of mechanical things also resulted in him making a number of interesting toys for me. One in particular has stayed in my mind; it consisted of a lemonade bottle filled with water into which he put the small plastic diver from a cornflakes packet, having first attached a small float. When I tightened the stopper the diver sank to the bottom, when I released the stopper he rose up again. A simple toy, difficult to make, but it provided many hours of entertainment for me.

Another great interest of my father's was photography. He had two cameras, a Box Brownie and a Kodak Folding Autographic. The latter had been bought from Lowrie Work, a work colleague, some years earlier and had accompanied my father to India after the war. It was always taken when we went for a walk and, of course, like any father, he used it to take a lot of pictures of me growing up.

In the early '50s flash photography was in its infancy and father decided that he would like to try it because it would allow him to take pictures inside. Unfortunately, his camera couldn't be adapted to synchronise a flash to the camera, and in any case he probably couldn't afford to purchase the flashguns available at the time, so he made his own. This consisted of an old reflector taken from a truck headlamp, with the bulb holder still attached. Into this he inserted the flashbulb holder. A short length of wire from the bulb holder, a 4½-volt 'flat' battery, and a small switch completed the home-made unit.

I have a great many photographs of family and friends that were taken in Garden Cottage using his home-made flashgun. The procedure was a little more complicated than it is today and went like this:

1. Decide where your subjects are going to stand or sit.
2. Set the camera up on a stable surface, tripod, table, chair etc. and frame the shot.
3. Measure the distance from the film plane on the camera to the subjects.
4. Transfer this figure to the calculator supplied by the flashbulb manufacturer to ascertain the aperture and set this on the camera.
5. Check that a flashbulb has been put in the flashgun and take the operating switch in your hand. Make sure that you know where the shutter button is!
6. Get an assistant to switch off the room lights.
7. Open the camera shutter.
8. Fire the flash.

Entertainments and Hobbies 63

9. *Close the shutter (otherwise the picture would be ruined when the lights came back on).*
10. *Put the lights back on.*

The resulting photographs were clear and sharp, but because the house lights had been switched off all the subjects' pupils were dilated.

Initially the flashbulbs were unprotected and sometimes they exploded, showering small fragments of glass everywhere. This problem was overcome by coating them in an early plastic, which had a bluish tinge; this acted as a filter and made the colour temperature of the flash light similar to that of daylight. The plastic melted when the flashbulb was fired and gave off a smell that I can still recall today.

One Christmas, Santa Claus brought me a Meccano set. Father helped me to make lots of different things with the set, including a simple, but very absorbing toy – an electric car!

The dilated pupil effect on both animal and human caused by taking a flash photograph in total darkness, mid 1950s. **Photo: Willie Smith**

He came home from Lerwick one night with a small electric motor that ran off a 4½-volt 'flat' battery. He bolted the motor to a flat piece of Meccano, fitted two axles with four wheels and a drive wheel to the back axle, and then built a 'car' body on top. The resulting 'car' ran for hours on one battery. I used to take it out onto the road in front of our house and play with it for hours and hours until the battery ran out. When it did I had to wait until someone bought me a new one before I could use my 'car' again.

As a stopgap measure, father showed me how to connect partially exhausted batteries from various torches etc. together, until I got enough power to drive my 'car'. I have to say that once or twice torches were found to have 'exhausted' their batteries much sooner than expected, but, of course, I knew nothing about that!

Margaret Janet Work, known to all as Marjory Work, lived next door to my grandparents at Stove and taught music at the Sandwick School. She knew that I was interested in photography and so, having cleared it with my parents, asked me if I would like to come to her house and see how pictures were made.

Marjory's father had been the local postmaster, and the house in which she lived, the post office. There were several big empty rooms that at one time must have been where they sorted the mail etc. It was in one of these that Marjory had set up a sink with a large draining board.

The first night I was there she showed me, using a roll of negatives and a developing tank, how the film had to be taken out of the camera and transferred on to the spool of the developing tank in total darkness. The next thing that had to be done was the preparation of the chemicals – developer, stop bath and fixer; the important thing about these is the control of the temperature; this didn't prove very easy in the large open room. However, by moving around paraffin heaters, control was at last achieved and developing of the film commenced.

At that time most cameras used a film that produced a negative 2¼ x 3¼ inches. Marjory had progressed to the 35mm variety. Once the film had been loaded into the developing tank in total darkness, then the lights could be switched on and the chemicals poured in and out as per the instructions. On completion, the film was checked to see if the negatives had been correctly exposed and would be printable.

Thirty-five mm film doesn't produce a very big image so an enlarger is required to get pictures of a suitable size to look at, or to make enlargements of a really good image. Marjory had acquired an enlarger that was capable of producing postcard-size prints without all the usual focussing etc. It consisted of a plastic box with a mount on one end to hold the film, and a drawer at the other end to take the paper, which again had to be loaded in total darkness. We were to use this on my next visit.

I went back to Marjory's a week later eager to see what the enlarged pictures would look like. The chemicals were mixed up and poured into three trays as before; developer, stop and fixer. The negative to be enlarged was selected and the paper taken out of its box and placed in the drawer, in total darkness. The light to expose the image was a 100-watt bulb which Marjory had previously arranged so that it hung just above the enlarger and could be switched on and off, by means of a switch, for the required few seconds. That done, the exposed paper was taken out and placed in the developer – this could be done using a 'safe light' – then we stood there waiting for the image to appear.

Now, in her haste to get everything arranged for my arrival, Marjory hadn't read the instructions as carefully as she should have done, for as we stood there, the image began to appear, but superimposed on top of it were the words OSRAM 100 WATT in a neat circle. We laughed our heads off, then turned the bulb on its side and proceeded to produce satisfactory postcards, many of which I still have today.

I loved my visits to Marjory. As well as teaching me about developing and printing pictures she also taught me how to play chess. I doubt very much if she would have been allowed to take a pupil to her house today, indulge in the black art of mixing up chemicals, and work with him in the dark! How times have changed.

Marjory Work, music teacher, chess player and photographer.
Photo: R. H. Ramsay

Aggie and Jean Harper

Living next door to us in Hoswick were Aggie and Jean Harper. Jean's mother, Isabella Jane Malcolmson Smith, was a sister to Willie a' Milton and the fourth member of the family. She married Laurence Harper on 10th January, 1923. On 1st May, 1927, Jane gave birth to a daughter, also called Jane, but throughout her life known as Jean. Unfortunately, Jane senior died of complications just four hours after her daughter was born, leaving her to be brought up by her father, Laurence, and his sister Agnes, known as Aggie.

Sadly, Laurence Harper died on 7th July, 1939, at just 42 years of age, leaving his 12-year-old daughter Jean an orphan, to be looked after by Aggie.

This was the second tragedy suffered by the Smith family of Milton. Margaret Smith, the third member of the family, was married to Stanley Sothcott, who came from the Isle of Wight. She died of tuberculosis in September, 1925, just three months after she had given birth to a son, Stanley Milton Sothcott. Joan Smith, the eldest of the Smith family, moved to the Sothcott family home in Ayrshire to help Stanley senior bring up his son, Milton.

Aggie and Jean's house still had the traditional flagstone floor with the odd daisy growing between the cracks. They had a dog called Spot, several cats, and a few hens. As a small boy I enjoyed visiting them, especially when there were young kittens and chickens to be seen. One day Aggie told me to, "Come doon da morn aboot 11 an I'll shaw dee something du's no seen afore."

Agnes Harper (Aggie) with her niece, Jane Harper (known as Jean).

Next morning I could hardly wait until 11 o'clock, wondering what Aggie had that she had not shown me already.

When I arrived, Aggie was waiting for me and she headed straight for the hen house. I knew that she had a hen sitting on eggs and thought that the chickens must have hatched. Not so, when we got inside the hen was still sitting. Aggie put her hand under her and took out an egg.

She went over to the door, where a small hole had been left when the natural knot in the wood had dried up and fallen out, and holding the egg up to the hole she said, "Come an see dis."

I ran over and there, inside the egg, I could clearly see movement; a head and a beak.

Seeing something like that at the age of four is impressive and is far more educational than any book.

"Dis time da morn he'll be hatched oot," Aggie said, putting the egg back.

I could hardly get home fast enough to tell my mother what I had seen. Next day I went back to see if the chick had hatched; sure enough he was there with several others as well.

Over the years I learned a lot from watching and listening to Aggie. She was particularly good at building a peat stack so that the rain ran off and didn't soak inside.

At the back of her house there were a number of gooseberry and raspberry bushes which all the young boys, me included, were partial to when they were ripe. We got chased many times, and rightly so, for we were in effect stealing a valuable food source that would be made into jam for use over the winter.

Aggie's rhubarb jam with ginger was a speciality.

Immediately across from the bushes, on the other side of the small track, was a ditch into which ran a continuous supply of water from a spring higher up the hill. This was known by all in Hoswick as 'Aggie's spoot'. We used it to wash tatties and fish, and also carried water from there to wash the windows or concrete round our house.

Like all those of her generation, Aggie had seen really hard times and struggled to get through them whilst bringing up her niece at the same time. She was a beautiful hand knitter and passed on her knowledge willingly to many others, including my mother.

Aggie had a few sheep, and grew tatties, neeps and carrots for their own use, in a rig just below our house. Several women, including my mother, would go and help plant the tatties in the spring. I sometimes went and helped her during the tattie lifting holidays.

Jean Harper came to visit us most days. At the time, she worked in the Sandwick Baking Company before moving to L. J. Smith's at Hoswick. She was very keen on amateur dramatics and won many prizes at the local drama festivals despite being a nervous wreck before going on stage.

Numerous rehearsals were held in our house, my father taking pictures as various scenes were enacted. I still have those pictures, some of which I'm sure the participants would feel very embarrassed about today!

Harold (Frank) Mathews

Harold Mathews was born in London in 1899. He met Jane W. Duncan, known locally as Jeannie Duncan (my father's first cousin), at the Gaiety Theatre in London one night during the war years. They started a relationship and, Harold having divorced his first wife, were married in the registrar's office in Lewisham on 10th July, 1947.

They moved to Shetland where in a small place like Sandwick a Londoner stuck out like a sore thumb. Strangers to these islands are often ridiculed and made fun of at every opportunity; Harold was no exception. For example, not long after he came to Shetland he went into a local shop and asked for "a packet of Players" (cigarettes) and was handed a pair of pliers! *The Two Ronnies* used the difference in speech to great effect when they did a memorable TV sketch many years later using "fork handles / four candles". Frank took all the ribbing in good humour and on many occasions made fun of himself.

How did he get the name Frank?

During the war, some misdemeanour or other was done and the whole company of men in which Harold served had their leave cancelled because no one would confess to the wrongdoing. Harold considered this to be unfair on him and his colleagues so he asked to speak to the commanding officer in private.

What he said I don't know, but on returning to the men with the officer, the officer told his section, "As a result of my discussion with Harold you are no longer under suspicion and are free to go on leave." He turned to Harold and thanked him for being "frank and honest", and the name stuck.

Harold (Frank) Mathews

Frank, as I will call him from now on, tried many things to make a living including running a small shop at Leebitton (the sign above the door read Frank H Mathews). From there, he organised events to try and bring custom to his shop, things like the round Sandwick race. His most ambitious project was his 'Come to Cumlie' effort at creating a pleasure beach.

In 1958, he rented the Cumliewick Beach for £3 from the laird. He parked two old buses on the back of the beach in which teas, cakes, ice cream and sandwiches were served. Several canoes were available for hire, there were swings, and even a photographer to record the events. Shetland isn't the most suitable place for such a venture and after two years it was abandoned.

Frank was keen on swimming and it was to be many years after his death before I was to find out exactly why. I remember him officiating at various swimming events including the tub race at the Sandwick regattas. On one occasion my father lined him up for a photograph and just at the critical moment Frank fell backwards, megaphone in hand, father pressed the shutter and a memorable photograph was in the bag.

Jeannie Mathews (née Duncan) with the Sandlodge bulldog. Photographer unknown.

Frank and Jeannie Mathews on their wedding day. Photographer unknown.

72   HOSWICK MAN

"COME TO CUMLIE"

This safe clean sandy Beach is now open for your enjoyment, come along any day between 10 a.m and 10.p.m for a swim or hire a Boat or relax in a Deck-Chair to watch the Swimming and Diving from the Raft.

Ideal ror Outings with swings for the younger folk.
Swimming Instructor and Photographer in daily attendance.
Light Refreshments, minerals, Ices, etc
Car Park at Broonies Taing.

COME TO CUMLIE
𝔉𝔯𝔞𝔫𝔧 𝔐𝔞𝔱𝔥𝔢𝔴𝔰
SANDWICK.

Above left: *Frank 'H' Mathews takes a tumble at the Sandwick regatta.*

Above right: *Handbill advertising the facilities at Broonies Taing. Note the printing error!*

Below: *Frank Mathews in one of the old buses used for serving tea, etc., at Broonies Taing.*
Photos: Willie Smith

Harold (Frank) Mathews

Above: One of the buses that Frank Mathews used for his 'Come to Cumlie' venture in 1958/59. **Photo: Martin Smith**

Below: Andrina Smith and Jeannie Mathews outside one of the buses at Broonies Taing. Judging from their clothing it must have been a typical Shetland summer day!
Photo: Willie Smith

74 Hoswick Man

Right: Trying out the swings next to Frank Mathews shop at Leebotten on regatta day.

Below: William Smith on the swings 1958/59.   **Photos: Willie Smith**

Below right: A canoe at Broonies Taing.

Bottom: Willie Smith and Jean Isbister try out the swings at Broonies Taing.
Photos: Martin Smith

In time Frank was accepted into the community and amongst other things became a member of the local coastguard unit, taking his turn on watch at the top of the Wart hill. Similar lookout posts were manned all round Shetland during bad weather to ensure the safety of mariners.

Jeannie spent all her life working for various lairds at Sandlodge, Lunna, Sumburgh and Edinburgh. In the early years this involved moving the entire household from Sandlodge to Lunna, where they spent the summer months, before moving back to Sandlodge for the winter. As you can imagine, she had many stories to tell, a number of them recorded by the Sandwick History Group before she passed away.

One story that she told me several times concerns the laird, Mr Wingate. He owned a bulldog which Jeannie loved and used to take for walks. On occasions when Mr Wingate went away on business, Jeannie would take the dog home and look after it. She recalled one night going out for a walk and meeting Mr Wingate with the dog. He stopped to talk to her and let her pet the dog. During the conversation Jeannie got the distinct impression that there was something serious on Mr Wingate's mind. Her concerns were proved right when, the very next morning, he took his own life.

The whole Smith family would go over to Frank and Jeannie's on Sandwick regatta day. This was a great occasion for a young boy like me to see and photograph. Sailing boats came from Lerwick and elsewhere to take part in the races; the Sandlodge boat took people for trips to Mousa.

Regatta day at Sandwick, sports on the Sandlodge green. **Photo: Martin Smith**

Above: Sandwick regatta day. **Photo: Willie Smith**

Below: One of the canoes for hire at Frank Mathew's Cumliewick pleasure beach.
Photo: Martin Smith

The laird's yacht was anchored on the start/finish line from where those invited on board could get a first-class view of the various events.

In the afternoon I took pictures of the field sports and, although cameras at the time didn't have the fast shutter speeds that they do today, I managed to get some memorable shots.

Frank passed away in 1973 and his widow Jeannie in 2000. It was whilst cleaning out their house that Frank's medals were found, together with instructions as to what he wanted done with them.

Included amongst the war medals were two medals for the 'All London Schools Swimming Champion' – one Harold Mathews.

I never heard him speak about winning those medals but no doubt they were the reason for his interest in swimming and beaches in Shetland. It was with pleasure that they were returned to his nephew, as he had wished all those years before.

Learning to Cycle

The first bicycle that I had was sent home to Shetland from Aberdeen by my uncle, James Mouat. Jimmy Mouat was a merchant seaman and on one of his trips home he said to my father that he thought it was time I had a bike. Father agreed, and Uncle Jimmy said he would have a look at what was available in Aberdeen on the way back to his ship.

Two days later, on 8th July, 1959, a telegram arrived advising that a bike was on the north boat.

It was with great excitement that I went with my father to the steamer's store on Friday morning and there, sure enough, was a bike with my name on the tally. It was loaded on board the Central van and taken home. The cost – £3 10/- (£3.50).

Naturally I was keen to learn how to cycle but stabilisers for bikes hadn't been thought about so I needed someone to steady me as I tried to get my balance. Father started to teach me and my pals also helped. After about a week of practice, I thought I was ready to go solo and so, as my mother looked on, I set off. All went well for 20 or 30 yards until I lost my balance and headed for the ditch, which unfortunately was full of nettles!

I landed amongst them clad only in short trousers and a short-sleeved shirt. It wasn't long before I was screaming in pain, the nettle stings hurting much more than the skinned knee. Our neighbour, old Leebie Youngclause, heard the commutation and came out to see what had happened. When she saw where my bike was lying and the state of my legs and arms she knew at once what was wrong. She gathered up some docken blades, crushed them in her hands to release the sap inside and rubbed this all over my legs and arms, that by now were very red and sore.

Soon the docken leaves did the trick and I stopped crying. An old remedy, but one that works, and was used any number of times after that whenever anybody got stung with nettles.

Old Leebie and her husband, Johnnie, were a great help to my mother, particularly in the early days after my birth, often hanging out the washing, including my nappies, because my mother wasn't able after her caesarean operation.

When I was old enough, I used to go to the shop and get errands for 'Auntie Leebie', who would give me two sugar lumps when I returned – no sweeties in the early '50s.

I finally got the hang of my bike and this opened up a much bigger area for me. I could go and visit my grandparents at Rocklea whenever I wanted, or go to the shops at Stove or the Central, for messages for my mother or to meet my father at the end of his working day. I never took my bike to school and can't recall anyone else from Hoswick doing so either.

As time went on I became more and more confident and finished up doing what all the rest of the boys did – we'd cycle up to the top of the hill to the south of Hoswick (known as the 'Sooth Ness'), turn the bike around, then pedal like crazy for the first 50 or so yards, take our hands off the handlebars, and use our weight to steer the bike the rest of the way down the hill and round the corner at the bottom.

This was later improved upon by taking our feet off the pedals as well!

I have to confess that I did both on a number of occasions until one day, as I rounded the corner, I met the Sandwich bus coming the other way! I had a choice – the front of the bus or a peat stack – I chose the peat stack. Fortunately for me, the peaty earth was soft, which slowed the bike up before it actually hit the stack so neither it nor I sustained any damage.

I soon realised that I had had a lucky escape from a very nasty accident or worse and never tried that stunt again.

Christmas and New Year

Like all young children I went guizing for pennies at Christmas, sometimes on my own and sometimes with others. Nobody had very much money so we didn't expect anything other than a penny or two. However, there was one house were they had two soup plates on the dresser – one was full of threepenny bits, the other silver sixpences. Naturally, we were keen to get there before they went to bed!

I was a very lucky young man because Santa Claus came to visit me at Garden Cottage, and also at Rocklea, the home of my grandparents and my great-grandmother. He brought me many fine things, some of which I still have today because in those days toys were extremely well made. It's worth mentioning that as well as toys, Santa brought an apple and an orange, something you maybe didn't see again until next Christmas.

Mother, father and I always had our Christmas dinner at Rocklea, usually around two o'clock, because my grandfather was a postman and he had to make deliveries on Christmas Day, just like any other. I say just like any other day but, of course, the kind folk of Sandwick all wanted to give him and the other postmen a dram on Christmas Day.

He always made it home in good spirits in time for his Christmas dinner and the home-made Christmas pudding. Great-grandmother Andrina always made the Christmas pudding. Her daughter Chrissie would gather all the ingredients together and then leave her to mix them and make everything ready. Several real silver sixpences were put in and there was great fun finding them all, before we began to eat, in case any were swallowed!

Some years after Andrina's death I found the recipe for the Christmas pudding, all measured out in handfuls owing to the fact that she was blind.

After dinner I would play with whatever Santa had brought me and later on granny would play the organ and we would all sing carols. Sometimes guizers would come along and we would have fun trying to guess who they were. Several brought fiddles or accordions and would give us a tune or two before moving on to the next house. Granny joined in on the organ whenever she could.

No artificial trees in my young days so nearly every house had a real one. Jean Harper, our neighbour from next door in Hoswick, always came to Garden Cottage to give us a hand to decorate ours. Jean and my father were first cousins. Both had a great sense of humour so there was much hilarity before the decorated tree was finally lit; much of it centred on the fairy and just exactly who was going to put her where!

Jean was very fond of me and looked after me on many occasions when my parents went to Lerwick or to a function in a local hall. She always wanted to know how I was getting on at school and encouraged me to read to her and show her how I did my sums. I'm sure I learned a great deal from her one way or another.

It wasn't only the young who went guizing at Christmas and the New Year; anything from eight to twelve men and women, maybe more, would go around the houses in groups or squads. Some came with a fiddle player and some with an accordionist. These 'squads' usually arrived at Garden Cottage via Peter Barclay's. Peter was a very generous host so they were usually in good fettle by the time they came to us.

We had a small porch that was just ideal for dancing in, it had four wood covered walls with no shelves and polished wax cloth on the floor. Jean Ganson was a popular local accordionist who played whilst many an eightsome reel was danced in our porch. On one occasion, when the squad decided that it was time to move on they all trouped out of the house, down the path, followed by Jean still playing her accordion. Unfortunately, she couldn't see that someone had shut the gate and so she, accordion and all, went head-first right over it! Fortunately, both survived to move on to the next house.

Beachcombing

Most of the Hoswick beach can be seen from Garden Cottage. I loved to play on the beach and, if the weather was fine, I would be allowed to go there provided I didn't go out of sight of our house. This was great fun, I would find all kinds of shells, crabs, brightly coloured stones, bits of wood, broken fish boxes and the thousand and one other things that came with the sea, including a particular type of white tube made of a material that was not known to me at the time. I found out that if I lit a small fire it caught fire easily and burned slowly giving off acrid black smoke and dripping just like a candle. Some years later I was to discover exactly where it had come from, exactly what it was for, and go on to sell many hundreds of them.

During the winter severe gales would send huge waves crashing onto the beach. I spent many hours watching them roll up and over the back of the beach on to the land behind. As the undertow ran back down you could hear the sound of millions of pebbles being dragged back. This continual pounding meant that the beach was littered with well-rounded pebbles, many of them white quartz. Then one year, after a particularly severe storm, the pebbles disappeared and were replaced with sand. This remained for several years until another gale removed the sand and returned the pebbles. I have been told that had I been able to see what had happened, I would have found the pebbles several hundred yards offshore and vice-versa.

At the east end of the beach there was a burn that ran into the sea. I caught several trout here by staking lines with a worm on a hook into the soft bank, some way back from the burn mouth, and leaving them overnight. Any fish that were caught remained out of sight of birds and prying eyes until I returned to collect them the next day.

I was always surprised to find small black eels in the burn at certain times of the year and didn't find out until I was much older that they come here all the way from the Sargasso Sea, a most incredible journey. Little did I know that I was to come into contact with their much larger brothers and sisters some years later.

So much for the enjoyment of a small boy; the Hoswick Beach and the surrounding areas had another part to play, this time in the lives of the adults, especially during and after a south-east gale. Such gales brought driftwood, or sometimes a deck cargo of sawn timbers lost overboard from a ship on passage from Norway or Russia. Some men used commercially-made torches for sighting their quarry at night, others made their own high-powered versions with a longer battery life that could pick out incoming battens from a much greater distance. It wasn't uncommon to see several torches going along the beach or the cliff tops during a stormy night. Every man carried a line with a grapnel hook attached for throwing over the wooden battens and dragging them ashore.

During my time in Hoswick, two deck cargos were driven ashore. The amount of timber involved enabled several men to gather enough to build new porches, outhouses etc. In true smuggling style, it was all spirited away by tractor and trailer before the Receiver of Wreck got to know about it.

Of course, not all the wood driven ashore was suitable for use as building material; a lot of it came in the form of broken fish-boxes, pond boards, masts, spars, or maybe even the remains of some unfortunate ship that had sunk and been broken up by the action of the sea. This was gathered up and placed in piles to be taken home later, dried, and then used as firewood.

Not all the things found on a beach are useful. One particular substance that appeared on the Hoswick beach on a number of occasions was brown in colour, round, and sometimes coated in small stones and other debris – I called them tar balls – they were in fact globules of heavy oils pumped overboard from the bilges of passing ships. Unfortunately, because they were sometimes under the sand or seaweed and couldn't be seen, folk going to the beach stepped on them and covered their footwear in the thick gungy mess, which took some removing as you can imagine.

It is common practice in Shetland, as elsewhere, to kill sheep and lambs and salt their flesh for the winter. This was usually done in late October or early November, the offal and the heads being dumped in the sea. With no refuse collection system, all household waste was also dumped on the beach to be removed by the in-coming tide. So, sometimes when I went to the beach on a lovely moonlit hairst night to dump our rubbish, I became aware of eyes looking back at me from the shallows! Some days later I would find the skulls picked clean by crabs and birds and washed white by the sea.

During the building of the early warning station at Mossy Hill you could get excellent views of what was going on from the Hoswick beach. The huge dishes that formed part of the station were, if my memory serves me right, taken up the hill in sections, bolted together and then heaved up into their vertical position.

It has always amused me that at a time when the Cold War was very much in evidence, whenever a dish was being raised on Mossy Hill a Russian trawler would seek shelter in Levenwick. I have been told that in order to do that, permission would have to have been obtained by the Russian Embassy from the British authorities. I often wonder if the person giving the permission had any idea where Mossy Hill was in relation to Levenwick, or just how good the view was of what was going on up there from the anchorage.

Going to School

I started my education at the Sandwick School in 1953. Every morning, some 20 children ranging in ages from five to 15 walked up the road from Hoswick, took a short cut through Jimmy Halcrow's croft, fed the grise (pig) some grass or dandelion leaves, then carried on up past the quarry behind Halcrow's shop, past the Free Kirk and on to the school.

Once there, lessons began. In the very early days these involved, amongst other things, Lexicon playing cards (a game similar to Scrabble, using cards) that were laid out on the table and you were taught the sound that each letter made. Once you had learned the sound of the letters, they were put into simple words – DOG, CAT, etc. – and each of us in turn had to say what the words were. If we couldn't then we had to sound out the letters to arrive at the correct word. As time went on the words got bigger and in time the cards were replaced with story books.

At the age of five, school days could sometimes drag, especially when the weather was fine and you could see your house from the classroom. However, in general the teachers were very good at keeping us amused whilst at the same time educating us until it was time to go home.

I was born left-handed, and even before I started school my parents had been told that writing with the left hand would not be allowed. Thinking that they were doing the right thing, they tried to teach me how to use my right hand before I went to school. This was totally against my natural instincts and led to many tearful outbursts on my part.

However, by the time I was ready to start school I was more-or-less right-handed. From time to time I opted for the left hand and, if caught, usually got a sharp reminder with a ruler across my knuckles. Not a very nice thing to do to a small child but I managed to make the change which proved very useful in later life.

Why were young children forced to change from their natural left hand to their right? No one has ever given me a definitive answer. As far as my teachers at the Sandwick school were concerned, my personal opinion is that they were old and set in their ways.

(Note: When I was in my forties I met Vera Johnson who lived at Leebotten. Vera was by profession a qualified chemist, who unfortunately had a very bad stammer. She, too, had been born left-handed and forced to change. In her opinion, and with the benefit of her medical knowledge, she was convinced that this had caused her affliction.)

The school day over, we started the journey home, either by reversing the route mentioned above (including feeding the grise!) or, by going via the Sandwick Baking Company shop to get a sweetie or a Lucky Bag to take home. Sometimes I went to my grandparents' house at Rocklea, then on to the shop, then home.

Without actually realising it the daily walk to the school was in itself educational because in the spring time you saw all the flowers come into bloom, the new born lambs in the fields, the muck being spread, and the fields being ploughed and planted. As the year went on you saw the crops come up, neeps singled, and tattie rows hoed to remove the weeds. Later on the hay was cut, and then the corn, and finally the tatties and neeps were taken up. Schools actually had holidays, supposedly to allow the children to help with the tattie lifting.

All this gave you a good insight into what life was about, where your food came from, and the amount of work that went into its production. During the summer holidays the older boys used to help take home the peats, often staying with a truck all day as it went from one customer to the next. The extra hands were much appreciated and usually rewarded with a few pennies.

Personally, I wasn't very involved with either peats or tatties because we didn't have any land, and I was still only a young boy. However, I did give Aggie Harper a hand during the tattie lifting holidays, and Mary Ann Sinclair, who had the rigs directly below our house, a hand with her hay and corn. In addition to her croft, Mary Ann also worked as a cook in the school canteen that kept us well fed during our early years. My favourite dinner was, and still is, fish and tatties followed by apple crumble

At the end of my first summer holidays spent working at Shetland Seafoods, I bought a Sobell all transistor radio as a memento of my first 'real work' and took it down to show Mary Ann, who was working in her hay. Together we listened to the weather forecast; she was just amazed that such a small box could pick up the forecast in the rigs outside. I still have that radio and it can still pick up the forecast!

Going to the school in the winter time was a different thing altogether. With no school bus to take us there, we had to make the same journey as we did any other day. The older children looked out for the smaller ones and helped them along the way, particularly if there was a gale of wind, or snow, or both. On arrival at the school we got off our coats, scarfs, and gloves, and went into the classrooms. These were usually lovely and warm, the cast iron radiators so hot that you could barely touch them.

If it began to snow heavily and there was a risk that it would continue for several hours then the decision would be taken to close the school and send us all home. Jimmy Willie Smith would arrive with the big red van belonging to L. J. Smith's shop at Hoswick and lift each one of us in turn into the back. When he had got us all in he would tell us to sit down and not move until we got to Hoswick. Then he pulled down the roller shutter door leaving us sitting in the dark.

The journey home was uneventful and on arrival at Hoswick, Jimmy Willie made sure that we all got home safely. If our parents were away for any reason he made sure that someone else took us in. As the years went on vehicles improved, and so my last trip was made in a van with a light in the back! Jimmy Willie made many such trips which were greatly appreciated by our parents. At the time we just took it all in our stride and looked on it at as a bit of fun.

As the 'Eleven Plus' exam approached, thoughts turned to the secondary school and then to what kind of work you might want to do when you left school. Fairly early on I decided that I would like to do a commercial course. Sandwick didn't provide such a course so the only option was to go to school in Lerwick, which involved a daily round trip by bus of some 30 miles.

For most people this wouldn't have presented a problem; unfortunately I suffered badly from motion sickness so the first week that I travelled to school in Lerwick wasn't a very nice experience. The driver had to stop the bus and let me off at least three times on the way to Lerwick, and the same on the way back at night. By the end of the week I was quite ill and my parents said that I would need to consider coming back to the Sandwick School.

I had always wanted to do a commercial course and that was only available in Lerwick, so I said I was going to go back on Monday for another week to see how things went, if they didn't improve then I would come back to the Sandwick School.

On Monday morning I got on the bus as usual and never felt sick any more. I suppose that, like sea-sickness, my body had become accustomed to the movements of the bus. Before long I could sleep all the way to or from Lerwick and got so used to the motion of the bus, the various twists and turns, that I could almost tell exactly where we were without opening my eyes.

A number of other boys and girls travelling to school in Lerwick weren't so lucky; they also suffered from motion sickness but unfortunately never got over it. To their credit they put up with it for four years or more in order to complete their education and pursue their chosen careers.

Going to school in Lerwick meant an early start, because Hoswick was where the bus started from. I had to get up at seven or slightly earlier, have breakfast, and then go and wait at L. J. Smith's shop for the bus to come and pick me up, along with several others. This was alright in fine weather and, of course, you met and spoke to various people going to their work at 8 o'clock. In addition, the crofters were always up and about early tending to their sheep, new-born lambs etc., and on really fine spring mornings I would watch the Duncan boy's tumbler pigeons displaying overhead.

There was always a lot to see on the trips to and from Lerwick in the 1960s. In the spring there were lots of rabbits chasing each other on the new grass in the Cliffs of Cunningsburgh. If you looked to the south or southeast, the vast fleet of Russian ships that were fishing around our shores at the time could be seen on the horizon as the sun came up behind them. Then, as with our walks to school in Sandwick, there was the complete crofting cycle of muck spreading, ploughing, sowing, haymaking, cutting corn etc. As the year went on it was interesting to see when different crofters did the various jobs; some were on the ball, others weren't in a hurry. Some had the very latest machinery, whilst others continued with the old manual ways.

The winter time was very different. For a start it was dark when I got up and there could be snow and ice on the ground. If it came on a shower of rain or snow I had to find shelter in the lee of one of L. J. Smith's shop buildings or the Hoswick Gospel Hall next door until the bus arrived. Quite often I was soaking wet before I got on the bus. Of course, the other boys and girls who joined the bus en route had the same experience, because there were no bus shelters in those days.

We arrived at Lerwick about a quarter to nine, cold and damp, tired, and not really in the best frame of mind to start our lessons.

The school day finished at four o'clock and once again we had to wait outside until the bus came to pick us up and take us home. Because Hoswick was the last stop on the route, I got home most nights about five o'clock. This meant that, during the winter months, I left home in the dark and came home in the dark so I was always keen to get outside on Saturday morning to see what changes had taken place during the week.

I made the daily journey by bus to Lerwick for two years before my family's situation changed and I moved to Lerwick permanently.

The Sandwick Baking Company (The Bakeshop) Fire

My mother was one of those people who, from time to time, dream about things that will subsequently happen. Over the years there were many instances of this, but the one that I remember most vividly, because the event took place so soon after the dream, was the fire in June 1961 that destroyed the Sandwick Baking Company.

Early on that morning my father came into my bedroom and woke me up. He told me that my mother had had another one of her dreams. This time she had dreamt that the bakeshop was on fire. He had scoffed at this when she woke him up in a very distressed state.

We couldn't see the bakeshop from our house, but just in case there was anything in it father got up and looked out the window. To his horror, he could see smoke billowing up over the hill past the school. This worried him because his parents' house was next door to the bakeshop.

We got dressed and headed off on foot to see if granny and grandad were all right. When we got to L. J. Smith's shop at Hoswick we could see all the commotion, there were firemen everywhere and hoses running from the Hoswick burn up the road to the bakeshop, which the firemen confirmed was on fire. They also confirmed that the little cottage next door was in no danger.

It turned out that the local water supply couldn't produce enough water pressure for the firemen's hoses, so in order to get more water at a decent pressure they had dammed the Hoswick burn and were using their high pressure pumps to lift the water from there.

The rear of the Sandwick Baking Company after the fire in 1961.

Photo: Peter Bain

Father and I continued up the road safe in the knowledge that granny and grandad were okay, only to find, despite the fact they lived only 50 or 60 yards away, they had slept through it all!

We spent a few minutes with them and then returned to Garden Cottage to prepare for work and school and confirm to my mother that the bakeshop had indeed burned down. All she said was, "So you'll surely believe me noo."

I got ready to catch the bus to school in Lerwick but needless-to-say there wasn't much thought given to schoolwork that day. I couldn't wait to get home to go and see what was left of the bakeshop. Sadly, only the walls were left standing and they were cracked. The floor was littered with debris; burnt wood from the roof, swollen half-baked and burst tins of fruit, partially burnt counters and waterlogged packets of every kind of food you could mention lay everywhere; a scene of complete devastation.

This was a disaster for the owner and the whole community but for the small group of boys and girls that had gathered it was, of course, something we had not seen before. As we stood there gazing in through the large openings where once the shop windows had been, the owner, Peter Malcolmson, cleared away some of the debris from around the safe and, after a few attempts, got it open.

The front of the Sandwich Baking Company after the fire in 1961.

Photo: Peter Bain

What happened next was the most generous act of kindness I have ever witnessed, especially in the circumstances. He turned and approached the small group of boys and girls and from the cash box in his hands, he gave each one of us a few pennies or a threepenny bit, told us to be careful and not to go inside because we might get hurt.

My uncle, John Isbister, was the policeman on duty at Sandwick that morning. Some years later his son, Ian, married Eunice Malcolmson, grand-daughter of Peter Malcolmson, the owner of the Sandwick Baking Company.

What causes people to have dreams about forthcoming events has been the subject of scientific research and discussion for many years. Unfortunately, I have inherited the ability, which at times can be unnerving and very worrying, but I have never taken part in any attempt to explain the phenomenon; I just live with it.

Local Amenities

The village of Hoswick was made up of just over 40 houses when I was a boy. Next to Garden Cottage were the ruins of an old house, with several large white quartz stones lining each side of the flagstone path leading up to the 'front door'.

Behind the house there was a small path along which people walked to other parts of the village. On the opposite side to our house was a stone-built retaining wall, some four feet high, with a well-made flat stone drain underneath it. This took water from a spring in the hill that came out in a pipe, or 'spoot', behind Aggie Harper's, approximately 50 to 60 yards away. The drain continued on behind the houses next to ours, all the way to the burn that ran down from the hill to the sea.

Similar well-made stone drains ran next to all the roads and paths throughout Hoswick and discharged into the Hoswick burn and then on into the sea. These drains could be flushed by opening the gate valve on the small reservoir situated in the hill behind the village.

In the summer time, when the flow of water wasn't heavy, I used to block the drain behind our house and use the 20- or 30-yard dam to sail my boats in. In the winter time, after heavy rain or when the snow melted, I could hear the water rushing down the drain as I lay in my bed.

I have always wondered when these drains were built, so recently I spent some time in the Shetland Archives looking for information. I found that in 1907/08 several meetings were held in Hoswick to ascertain what type of drainage system the various businesses and homeowners would prefer. Eventually it was decided that an open drain system would be preferred.

The following are extracts from the minutes of the Zetland County Council Mainland District Committee:

> At a meeting of the Zetland County Council Mainland District Committee held on the 19th of March 1908 a plan and specification of the proposed drainage for Hoswick was laid on the table, and the sanitary inspector was directed to report there on to a future meeting.
>
> At the next meeting held on the 16th of April 1908 a report by the sanitary inspector on the plan and specification for the proposed drainage scheme to be carried out by the proprietors and inhabitants of Hoswick was read and the inspector having stated that he was satisfied with the scheme the meeting resolved to approve thereof.

The Shetland Times reported on the above meetings and said that the estimated cost of the scheme was £88.

Most of the original drains survive to this day, which says a lot about the skill of the men who subsequently built them.

In the early 1950s, seven street lights were installed in the village. The meter and time clock were installed in Jack Smith's garage, he collected the money (originally 2/6 rising to 3/- [12½ to 15p]) every quarter from each household to pay for the electricity. The seven lights soon became known as the 'Seven Sisters', after the constellation of the same name.

Street lighting was, of course, very useful to the whole community, it also came in very handy when we were sledging in the winter time. However, Cecil Duncan reminded me that we weren't always appreciative of the lights, for we sometimes tried to knock out the light bulb with snowballs if the glass cover had been broken leaving it exposed! The lights were turned off at midnight to save expense and because they weren't needed, certainly not for crime prevention!

There were no barber shops or ladies' hairdressers in Hoswick or Sandwick so it was common practice for the local women to cut, curl, perm, and colour each other's hair. Several women from Hoswick and other parts of Sandwick used to come to Garden Cottage on a regular basis to have their hair done, or to do my mother's.

The most common type of concoction used went by the name of TWINK, and to this day I can smell the very strong ammonia aroma that hung around our house for several days if there had been a perming session prior to a wedding!

Small boys whose parents couldn't cut their hair had it cut by Sammy Sinclair or Jimmy Willie Smith whilst sitting on a fish-box in their shed! Jimmy Willie sometimes wore goggles to stop little bits of wiry hair, like mine, getting in his eyes!

The lack of hairdressing facilities wasn't the only problem that had to be overcome by improvisation – dressmaking was another. One or two local women were renowned for the fact that they could make or alter dresses for special occasions.

Nobody had very much money in the early '50s so clothes were handed down or passed on to other children; these were altered to suit by your mother if she could do it, or given to someone who could.

My mother made many such alterations for me using a pre-war hand-operated sewing machine. As a result, the very beautiful song *Coat of Many Colours* by Dolly Parton, always brings a lump to my throat when I hear it and think of all the hard work she, and other women of the time, put in to ensure their children had decent clothes to go to school in.

Clothing a large family of five or six in the early '50s could not have been easy, and there were several families of that size in Hoswick at the time.

Sunday

In the mid-1950s Sunday was reserved for more religious pursuits than it is today.

Local man, Samuel Sinclair, was a lay preacher who held Sunday school for the Hoswick children in what was affectionately known as the 'Red Hall', owing to the fact the wooden building, which was situated directly behind L. J. Smith's shop, had a red roof. He also held evening services there for the adults. Concerts and special services were held at certain times of the year, e.g. harvest thanksgiving and Christmas.

One Christmas concert for the children sticks in my mind. Each one of us had to go to the front of the hall, recite a verse, and then place a wooden brick onto a structure. The smallest and youngest started first, and as each row of bricks got smaller they also got higher and were placed by the older and taller children. In time it could be seen that the construction was becoming a lighthouse.

The highlight came when Sammy placed a bulb in the light and switched it on. The message was, of course, that "God's light shines throughout the world." Very impressive when you were five years old and, as far as I am concerned, that simple service and its message have been remembered for over 50 years!

There were three other churches in Sandwick at the time – The Church of Scotland at Sannick, the Free Kirk, and the Wesleyan Chapel at Stove. A bus was laid on to take members of the congregation to the Big Kirk, as the Church of Scotland was known; smaller dormobiles collected the members of the other two faiths.

I can remember going by bus to a harvest thanksgiving service in the Big Kirk with my parents. The congregation was so big that we had to sit upstairs, three rows from the back, from where I watched a man ring the bell by pulling on a rope that hung down through a small hatch in the roof. Sadly, today's congregations are very much smaller and the last time I saw the Red Hall it was in very poor condition and was being used as a builder's store.

We had no television, leisure centres or social clubs in the mid-50s; very few people had their own cars and there was no bus service to Lerwick so travel outside the district was limited on a Sunday.

Fine Sundays were spent either playing or going for walks around Hoswick or Sandwick, visiting relatives and friends. My father used to take me for walks across the Hoswick burn, along the cliffs below Cullister and all the way to Broonies Taing. Just before we came to the pier, there lay a number of boat hulls in various states of decay. Father told me that his grandfather, 'Smiddy Magnie', had made the various metal fittings on them.

Having spent some time at Broonies Taing we would continue our walk back along the road, past the school, and finish up at Rocklea – granny and grandad's house – for a cup of tea before returning to Garden Cottage.

Two other walks that I enjoyed were to the Noost at Hoswick – or more correctly Mitchell's pier – where I got to sail boats made from newspaper; or up the hill above Hoswick from where you could see Swinister and Stove. Father always took his camera with him on these walks. The resulting photographs are now an excellent record, not only of my early childhood, but of the layout of Hoswick, Stove and other parts of Sandwick.

It was during one of these walks along the shore past Mitchell's pier that my father suggested I try and take his photograph. I took the Kodak No. 2 Folding Autographic Brownie from him and, after a little while, managed to get his image lined up in the small waist level viewfinder, which showed everything back to front. I pressed the shutter and, of course, didn't see the result until a few days later. When I did see it I was delighted; that photograph was to spark off a lifetime interest in photography.

No doubt my mother took advantage of the time we were away to catch up on housework and have some time to herself. Sometimes she would come with us, and it was on these occasions that some of the best photographs that I have of her were taken.

During the summer months Auntie Jean and Uncle John would come down from Lerwick and take us for runs in their Austin A35 car. These

Willie Smith photographed by his son, Martin. The first real photo taken by the author.

runs usually included an excellent picnic at a spot overlooking either the Spiggie beach or St Ninian's Isle. I loved Auntie Jean's home-made buns and today over 50 years later I still do!

School Holidays

Every young boy looks forward to his school holidays; I was no exception. At Easter holiday time the crofters in the district were starting to spread muck, ploughing, planting, and working with sheep and newly born lambs. If someone had a caddy lamb and you were given the chance to feed it that was really exciting.

When the weather wasn't fine we spent a lot of time in L. J. Smith's weaving sheds watching the men set up and operate the various machines. The setting up of the warp seemed to take several days, then the shuttles for the weft had to be filled from large cones on to the much smaller ones that went into the shuttles.

If we were really good then sometimes the men would allow us to do this job. We felt that we were really helping things along and were fascinated watching the finished cloth appearing as the machines were operated. The actual weaving machines were powered by two large metal pedals, which the men, sitting on stools, pushed all day long. It may have kept the men fit but it must have been a very tiring job – in effect walking all day every day for years.

I used to like watching John Youngclause, or Doonie as he was better known, working the hand loom to produce special cloth. How I wish now that I had been able to take pictures, or better still, videos of both operations.

The summer holidays lasted for seven weeks and in that time, with the better weather, there was a lot more to do. Exploring on the beach was a favourite of mine, as was fishing for sillicks at the Noost (Mitchell's pier).

Before you could start fishing you had to get your gear sorted. No fibreglass rods or fancy reels; all you had was a hook bought from L. J. Smith's shop, which you attached to a piece of thin string or heavy black cotton thread so the fish couldn't see it. Having done that you fashioned a loop on the other end to put your finger in, and then went looking for bait.

Whelks were picked off the rocks and limpets knocked off with a stone, their shells smashed to get at the flesh, which was cut into small pieces and attached to the hook. We all carried pocket-knives from a very early age, our parents having taught us how to use them properly. Uncle John taught me how to sharpen mine until I could shave the hairs off my arm with it.

We also looked for green crabs under the rocks. They were quickly dispatched with a stone, then dismembered and thrown in the sea to attract the sillicks.

Having got your line and bait ready, you picked your way carefully down the pier, which was usually covered in green growth and tang, and threw in your baited hook. The excitement grew as the sillicks approached your hook; if one took a bite you felt it instantly and gave the line a good yank to set in the hook. Once you had landed the first one you had another source of bait – the sillick's eyes! They were excellent bait because they flashed like mirrors under the water.

On occasion, we would buy a ball of string from the shop and use this to catch bigger crabs using the following method. Several limpets were tied together on one end of the string and a stone attached three or four feet back from them. Whilst one boy held the ball of string and payed it out slowly, another would scramble out over the rocks to where the water was deeper and the bottom sandy. This was usually done at low tide so that you could get the bait set further out. When there was no more string left the stone and limpets were thrown into the water, having first made sure that there were no obstacles between the drop-in point and the boy retrieving the line on the shore.

After a few minutes the line was retrieved very slowly. The moving bait would attract a crab's attention and it would dash out from under the rocks onto the sand, grab the bait, and try to get back to its lair as quickly as possible. But it couldn't do this as long as tension was kept on the line, and greed prevented it from letting go, so it continued walking with the bait in its claws.

If the crab did manage to get back to its lair you had either lost your string for good, or at least until the next low tide before you could recover it, so keeping a constant strain on the line and slowly winding it in was vital to success.

As the string was wound in you could tell by the level of excitement coming from the small boys watching from the rocks if there was a crab on the end of the line or not. If there was, you kept pulling in the line, if not you stopped pulling until a luckless crab had attached itself to the bait.

Once ashore, the crab was usually looked at in detail and compared in size to others that had been caught. Since this fishing was done when the tide was out the crabs were usually released around the pier and re-caught later for bait.

Sometimes if the older men had been off at the hand-line they would give us the bait that they hadn't used, and sometimes, if they had caught a lot of fish, some to take home and eat. That was a real treat and an illustration of how members of the community helped each other.

My grandfather, Willie a' Milton, would sometimes take me to fish for piltocks from the big pier at Broonie's Taing. We used bamboo poles (known locally as piltock waands), six to eight feet in length, with a line a few feet shorter attached. A flea with four to six hooks, with chicken feathers or pigs birse (hair) tied to them to attract the fish was attached to the line, and finally a small lead weight with hooks tied to it or moulded into it – called a 'murderer' – was tied on to the bottom of the flea. The weight ensured that the line, hooks and murderer all hung straight when you stood or sat on the pier and moved your waand gently up and down. This method has been used in Shetland for generations to catch piltocks, usually from the rocks or craigs.

We caught a lot of fish this way. Sometimes we had to stop fishing or we wouldn't have been able to carry it all home, and that would have meant throwing the surplus away, which was a waste, so it wasn't done. Another valuable lesson learnt early in life – only take what you can use; come back for the rest another day.

The piltocks were gutted and washed at Broonie's Taing before we set of for grandad's home at Rocklea. I would be given some fish to take home to Garden Cottage, the rest would either be eaten by my grandparents or salted and dried for use later.

My father got two weeks summer holidays and, having tarred the roof at Garden Cottage and painted the windows and doors, we would go to Annfield at Sand, on the westside, to visit my mother's parents, Adam and Ruby Ewenson. The journey was made in my early years on Jimmy Watt's bus, and took anything up to two hours. I suffered very badly from car sickness and was always ill whenever I travelled to Lerwick from Sandwick,

Thomson's, Smith's and Irvine's buses with Thomson's car at Burn Beach, Scalloway.
Photo: Willie Smith

but I can't recall ever having been ill on Jimmy Watt's bus, probably because it made so many stops!

Watt's bus was another lifeline for the people on the westside and although they may not have travelled to Lerwick in person, they sent orders to the shops either by letter, another passenger, or the bus driver himself. As a result the bus was laden with boxes of all shapes and sizes. At each stop a man or woman would be waiting to collect his or her box, which was duly handed over, and then the latest news from Lerwick imparted, all of which took several minutes.

When we arrived at Sand we would go first of all to Auntie Ethel's house at Chapelside, where granny and grandad would be waiting for us, and I could meet up with my cousins, Ronnie and June Mouat. Ronnie was good with his hands and made sailing boats out of old seven-pound jam tins. I, on the other hand, had usually visited Stove & Smith's or Goudie's and bought one.

After having something to eat we would walk from Chapelside to Annfield, over the hill. The first thing to come in sight was the top of the hydro pole – the last one on the line, and then the chimney pots, and finally Annfield itself, with that beautiful view of Sandsound on the other side, and the reflection in the sea of the hills all the way up Tresta Voe. What a place to spend a holiday.

Next day I would wake up to the smell of meths and paraffin coming from the Primus stove that grandad always lit first, so that he could make a cup of tea for him and granny before they set about cleaning out the stove and lighting it. Once that had been done, granny would set about preparing a hearty breakfast for everybody, after which it was time to explore. Grandad and granny had a few sheep and lambs that were so tame

Above: From left: June Mouat, Adam Ewenson, Martin Smith (the author) steering, and Ronnie Mouat.

Right: The author practises rowing with his cousin Ronnie Mouat, in Adam Ewenson's small boat at Annfield, Sand, mid 1950s.

Below: Discussing fishing gear at Annfield with Ronnie Mouat, 1950s. **Photos: Willie Smith**

they would come and eat the potato peelings out of your hand. Behind the house, in the upper yard they grew potatoes, and in the lower yard, which had trees growing all round it, more vegetables, mainly carrots and neeps (turnips).

Both yards were surrounded with stone walls and the gates protected with small mesh wire to stop the rabbits getting in. To the south of the lower yard there was a well that sometimes dried up in the summer. When that happened they used another one in the adjoining park. If both dried up there was yet another, right on top of the cliff below the house, known as 'da banks well'. It never dried up and when my mother was a child a trout was kept in it to keep the water clean.

Granny and grandad also kept a number of hens so they had plenty of eggs to eat and bake with. Once or twice during the summer months grandad would go to the island of Sanda and come back with several buckets of 'shell-sand' for the hens. As the name suggests the sand consisted of a high proportion of ground-up seashells. The hens gobbled it up and a few days later you could see a difference in the thickness of their egg shells and a much richer colour to the yolk. In order to preserve the eggs for use over the winter months they were dipped into a substance called water glass. This apparently sealed up the pores of the shell and prevented the eggs going off.

If the weather conditions were good at the right time of year, Grandad Adam and Uncle Jimmy Mouat would go to the outer isles and collect seagulls' eggs. These were tested in a jug of water to make sure that they were fresh. If they sank they were okay, if they floated it meant that they couldn't be used because incubation had started. The good eggs were used by granny to bake cakes, which as I recall tasted pretty good.

Granny Ruby was a very interesting woman who, like many more of her generation, knew all about nature and the seasons. She had a most unusual pet – she kept a frog! Now I don't know how many years frogs are supposed to live but this one was in Annfield before my mother married in 1945, and he was still there in 1956 when I was six, so he was at least 12 years old, maybe more. Two or three times a week he would be taken out of his bowl and placed on newspaper on the kitchen table for us to look at, whilst Granny went outside to dig up some worms. These were placed on the newspaper and it wasn't long before the frog caught and ate them one by one. Seeing that at such close quarters kept everybody, young and old alike, fascinated for many an hour or two.

Ronnie and June would come down to Annfield and we would all play together, either up at the house or, best of all, down at the noost where grandad kept the flit boat, the *Baabie*, which he had used for years to bring the peats home from Saltness. There were no sillicks around the noost because the water was too shallow, however, there were lots of hermit crabs. We spent many hours catching and playing with them and watching them fight over scraps we put in.

An adult would always accompany us to the noost as it was below a high bank and couldn't be seen from the house. Ronnie and I spent many hours sailing our boats down there. On occasion, we were allowed to set our boats out to sea across the voe, then grandad would take us in his small boat to follow them. This was a great thrill – sailing your boat on the 'open' sea.

When the weather and tides were right he would take us all off in the *Baabie* to fish for piltocks or mackerel. This was also a great thrill and meant that we all got a turn at steering the boat using the Anzani outboard motor. Most of the fishing was done using the 'dorro' – believe me, there was some excitement on board the *Baabie* when three youngsters and several adults all got into mackerel at the same time!

One time I was lucky enough to get six mackerel on my line and was doing well getting them to the stern of the boat when they saw the silver propeller and made a dash for it. Grandad looked at the ensuing tangle

The author and his cousin, Ronnie Mouat, sailing boats at Annfield, Sand.
Photo: Willie Smith

and decided that the only way he was going to be able to clear it was to lift the outboard inboard. It must have taken about 15 minutes to untangle the line, fish and propeller, all the time keeping small hands and feet away from the sprickling fish and the hooks. In due course calm was restored and we got on with the fishing once more.

Once or twice we used the fleas on piltock waands without the murderers. This meant that the fleas stayed on the surface. The boat's engine was started and put in slow-ahead, so that we could cover a wider area if the fish were moving fast and close to the surface, as they sometimes do in the summer months. If our luck was in, the mackerel and piltocks swam after the feathered hooks and grabbed them.

Both methods were successful and enough fish were taken home for us to eat and for some to be salted and dried in the traditional way. Granny was an excellent cook and next day we would have a dinner of fresh fish, new tatties from the rig, home-made butter and bread – delicious.

A year or two before I left school I spent a week on holiday with granny and grandad on my own. During the week, grandad mentioned that he had lost two hens to what he thought was wild cats or stoats. I have always been keen on nature and knew how the experts made and set traps to catch the various animals. I talked to grandad about this and we agreed to try and make a trap to catch whatever was killing and eating his hens.

I suppose it took us no more than half a day to make and set the trap, which was baited with a nice piece of fresh chicken, before we went to bed. Next morning there was nothing in the trap and, as it was my last day at Annfield, I left thinking that as I had failed to catch a cat or stoat I wouldn't be much use as a great white hunter.

Ruby and Adam didn't have a phone, so it was a week later – when they came to Lerwick to do some shopping – that I came home from school to be told by grandad, "Boy, dy trap wirked efter aa – a'm catched three cats so far!"

The Van Men

For many years the people in the country districts of Shetland relied on grocer, butcher and fish vans for their weekly supplies. In the 1950s and early 1960s very few people could afford their own cars, and bus trips to Lerwick were made only rarely, perhaps for a hospital appointment or to visit the dentist.

After a short time working in the Sandwick Baking Company's shop at Stove, Sandwick, my father became a van driver for George R. Jamieson & Sons, Central, Sandwick. He was with the company from May 1953 until December 1960. His route was mainly to the south end of Shetland, from Sandwick to the Sumburgh Head Lighthouse and all points in between.

A typical day would start with him getting up at half past six, having breakfast and then walking from Hoswick to the Central. The early part of the day would be spent checking the van itself, making sure there was enough fuel, oil, water in the radiator, and that the tyres were inflated and not damaged.

That done, the van had to be loaded up with all the items for sale. Tea, sugar and butter didn't come in fancy packets like they do today, it all had to be weighed, packed and priced beforehand, usually by the main shop staff. Tea came in wooden chests from the wholesalers and was weighed into quarter or half-pound bags; sugar into one-pound bags. The paper bags were brown and made for the purpose.

Butter came in barrels and had to be cut into portions of half a pound or a pound, squared up using butter pats, and wrapped in greaseproof

Above: Willie Smith in the Sandwick Baking Co. van.
Photo: Peter (Rumlie) Malcolmson

Below: Willie Smith with the Central van, outside Garden Cottage, Hoswick.
Photo: Martin Smith

Peter Malcolmson (Rumlie) in the bakeshop van. **Photo: Willie Smith**

paper. Likewise the cheese, which also came in a barrel, was cut into manageable sizes using a cheese wire (a length of wire with a wooden grip at each end), weighed and priced according to size.

Small amounts of medicines including milk of magnesia, aspirins, syrup of figs, and various kinds of cough medicine were kept on the van shelves. Cigarettes, tobacco, matches, and spare parts for Tilley lamps were also carried; the latter selling well during the winter months!

Finally, the perishable items like bread and butcher meat were loaded and final checks made to make sure that any special items that had been requested during the last trip hadn't been missed, for example, it wasn't uncommon to see a barrel of molasses being put on board for a farmer who wanted it for his cows.

In the summer time several gallons of Archangel tar and numerous brushes were carried to people for tarring the roofs of their houses. Molasses and tar weren't the best things to carry in a grocery van; they made a real mess if they leaked, which wasn't uncommon.

One old lady got a 'special item' every week – a half bottle of whisky for her rheumatism. If my father was going on holiday for two weeks this was increased to a full bottle because the other driver was an elder of the Big Kirk and couldn't be asked to bring her whisky!

Having got the van ready for the day's trip father would come to Hoswick for something to eat and pick up his 'piece box' and flask of tea. This he would have at some point during the afternoon, usually around tea time, because his day didn't finish until six or seven at night, sometimes later.

The customers were very kind to the van men and on many occasions they were asked into their houses for lunch or tea. This was a regular occurrence and was much appreciated by all the van men. Nothing better to set you up for the rest of your day's work than home-made bannocks and butter or a full Shetland lunch of home grown produce.

I suppose the customers relied on the vans, and the van men on them, so each was helping the other.

As a young boy, I went with my father in the van during most of my summer holidays. I got to know lots of people and witnessed many things that, today, I wish I had been able to photograph. For example, during the summer months people working their peats would wave to get the van to stop as it went past so that they could get lemonade, cigarettes, or bread to have during a break from their labours. At that time it was quite common to see horses being used to sledge the peats down from the peat banks to the road. In other places they used a system of pulleys and baskets.

The author, Martin Smith, with his father, Willie, and the Central van.
Photo: Adeline Smith

From left: Willie Smith, Bernard Manson and Andrew Duncan in the Central Bakery garage.

A lot happened in the crofting cycle as the summer went on; making hay, cutting corn, taking up tatties and neeps. I enjoyed seeing it all and sometimes there was enough time to go for a run on a tractor, or visit a byre at milking time, before we had to move on.

One particular thing I enjoyed was going to Hillwell, in Quendale, on a Saturday night. It was usually after tea before we got there and once the van was parked they opened the gate to let the cows walk up the road into the byre for milking. I watched this spectacle with great amusement and followed the cows into the byre, where I was usually handed a mug of milk straight out of the cooler – now you can't get fresher than that!

Another favourite run was to Wester Quarff. If the tide was out then I could go exploring on the beach and pick up all kinds of things, including cockleshells. The sand on that beach is dark in colour and it is the only place in Shetland where I have been able to pick up live cockles.

Once a man came to the van carrying the biggest gun I had ever seen. He proceeded to show us how he loaded it with powder, wadding, and finally a lead ball, for this was a muzzle loader. Having finished loading the gun he picked out a target and fired. That's the only time that I have seen a muzzle loader being used. Some weeks later he took us to his house and showed father and me the moulds that he used to make the different sizes of lead shot.

At this time, only some ten years had elapsed since the Second World War, during which many of the people we were seeing had gone through some very hard times. For example, one day we stopped at an old cottage and an elderly lady, dressed from head to toe in black, with strange marks on her face and hands, made her way to the van. I was a little frightened of her at first but soon got over this when she spoke.

"Whit can I get de da day?" father asked.

"Haes do ony o yon new metal mantle clocks?" asked the old lady.

"Yea, I hae dis new Westclox kind. Is di een come dune?" father asked.

"Da rats is aetin him till he's faain apo da floor," she replied.

For the benefit of those who don't read the Shetland dialect, the above conversation went something like this:

"What can I do for you today?"

"Do you have any of those new steel mantle clocks?"

"Yes, I have this new Westclox kind. Has your one become old and useless?"

"The rats have eaten my clock until it has fallen on the floor."

Father had always wondered what caused the strange marks on the old lady's face and hands. From that day on he was convinced that the rats had been biting her while she was asleep.

On another occasion I went exploring round a croft as I often did, looking for kittens, young dogs or caddy lambs. I heard a noise coming from a small outhouse and went inside for a look. The floor was covered in straw and there was a man on his hands and knees crawling amongst it. He stopped, picked up what looked like an empty bottle, tried to get the last little bit of liquid out of it, then threw it away and looked for another. This scared me, so I ran back to the safety of the van and waited in the cab for my father. When I told him what I had seen, he said that the man had been through hell during the war and that he had taken to drink as a result.

There were many other similar cases but none of them have left the impression on me that those two have done.

A more light-hearted memory revolves around the space race. On 4th October, 1957, the Russians won the space race by launching Sputnik 1, which orbited the earth for several days and lead to worldwide headlines.

Around this time, George R. Jamieson & Sons produced a pastry case filled with mince, tatties and peas. It was very popular, sold well, made a really good meal, and was immediately christened a Sputnik by the customers, after the Russian satellite.

The following summer when I went with my father in the van there was a lot of speculation whenever there was heavy rain, or the crops weren't growing right, as to whether or not it was due to "yon thing it da Russians pat up ida sky last year."

Up to now I have referred to these vehicles as 'vans', which was the term used by the public. The 'vans' were, in fact, truck chassis onto which a purpose-built unit had been fitted so that they could be used for their other, equally important job, of fetching all the goods needed for the owner's main shop and bakery from Lerwick, and to make deliveries of bread to both Lerwick and Scalloway.

My father made the trip to Lerwick via Scalloway twice a week, on Tuesday and Friday. Having delivered bread to the Scalloway shops and picked up the empty trays he would head off to the steamer's store in Lerwick to collect all kinds of hardware, scythe handles and blades, rakes, buckets, spades etc. The next stop was Tods, where he loaded chocolates, sweets of various kinds, biscuits in tins, and various kinds of meat in both large and small tins. The small tins were sold direct to the customers; the large ones were opened up in the shop and slices sold in varying amounts as required.

The heaviest item that came from Tods was the flour for making all the bread. This came in bough bags and was lowered down a chute from Commercial Street level on to the shoulders of my father, or one of Tod's men, below, then put in the van.

On one occasion I was watching this and noticed a man going around the store with a sail maker's needle and thread. "What's he doing with the needle and thread?" I asked.

Father smiled and said, "He's probably sewing up the rat holes in the flour bags."

This may have been the case or it may have been a joke put about by the van drivers, I don't know. I prefer to think that the bags had been torn during their handling and that they were being repaired to prevent the flour spilling out.

Next stop was Billy Bain's in Fort Road, where the van was loaded with more biscuits, vegetables and, in season, various kinds of fruit including apples, oranges and melons.

Loading complete, the van would be taken to Donnie Henderson, at what is now Grantfield Garage, for any repairs that were needed to the lights, engine or exhaust. That done the van headed for Sandwick.

These journeys were not without incident; breakdowns were common and some ingenuity was needed to get you home. One night one of the vans began to give trouble, losing power and misfiring. Knowing that there was another van not far behind him, the driver stopped and waited. Both drivers then tried to find the cause of the problem. Before long they found a punctured fuel line. They didn't have any fancy mending tape of the kind available now, so they made do with what they had – a large potato was acquired from the back of one of the vans, the fuel pipe broken in two and both ends inserted into the potato, which now acted like an in-line filter! The remaining part of the journey went without incident.

On arrival at Sandwick the van had to be unloaded, and the counter and any shelving etc. that had been removed replaced, ready for the Saturday trip to the Ness.

I enjoyed my many summer holiday trips in the Central van, and even today I speak to people I first met at the van all those years ago. Sadly, the years are taking their toll and the numbers are dwindling.

Winter was a different matter altogether for the van men. Heavy falls of snow were common and quite often my father would go out in the morning and not come home again for two or three days.

If there was snow on the ground before he left the Central then the chains could be put on, but if the roads were clear he couldn't because this

The Van Men 115

Above: Hoswick after a heavy snowfall in 1960. *Photo: Willie Smith*

Left: Digging out a big 'fan' of snow outside the Central. Front row: Andrew Duncan, Jimmy Sutherland and Willie Smith. *Photo: Billy Smith*

Below left: L. J. Smith (Jnr.) takes supplies to Hoswick by sledge after the delivery van got stuck.
Photo: Willie Smith

Below: After nine days without any mail all hands turn out to carry the mail bags over the snowdrift to the Post Office.
Photo: Billy Smith

wore the chains out and caused a lot of vibration. If it snowed later in the day then the chains had to be put on so that he could get round the various districts and back home again. It isn't easy trying to put cold metal chains on across the double back wheels of a vehicle when your hands are frozen, but all the van men had to do it at some time or another.

If the weather got too bad and the vans got stuck or went off the road, the drivers would be taken in by the local people nearby, fed and given shelter until the snowploughs got the roads open again, one or two days later.

Whilst all this was going on mother and I were at home. If it started to snow then obviously mother became concerned as to whether or not father would get home. We didn't have a phone – very few people did – so very often we didn't know what had happened until George R. Jamieson's contacted us the next day, or sent a message to the Hoswick shop if the Sandwick roads were blocked as well.

But within a day or two the roads would be cleared, the vans returned to base, and the whole process would start again.

More often than not when we got a blizzard that stopped the vans, we also lost the hydro power. That meant mother had to light the Tilley lamp so that we could see round the house. Of course, the loss of power meant that everybody else in the district had to do the same. It always amazes me that with small children running round there weren't any accidents or fires. It says a lot for our parents that they were able to cope in such situations.

I said at the beginning of this piece that for many years the people in the country districts of Shetland relied on grocer, butcher and fish vans for their weekly supplies. I would like to put on record my appreciation of the men who, like my father, provided this service to Hoswick, namely: Andrew Duncan (grocer); Magnus Smith (butcher); Joe Strachan (Co-op); Eric Halcrow (fish); Jackie Henderson (milk); and our postman Nicol Stove.

Nicol and Jackie were an excellent double act, full of fun and at the same time dedicated to getting the mail and milk to their customers. On bad days in the summer time Jackie would take Nicol with him in his van, and in the winter time the roles would be reversed. I remember one winter's day, Nicol turned up at Hoswick with his tractor and trailer loaded, not only with Jackie and the milk, but also the mail and assorted vegetables from his croft. Considering that the roads had been blocked for more than a week they were a very welcome sight.

A New Beginning

In 1960, my father was unwell and off work for some months. This coincided with a reduction in the number of vans that George R. Jamieson's operated so, after seven years and seven months with the company, he was paid off on 31st December, 1960.

Several months on the dole followed and then one night he spoke to Magnie Geordie Smith, who told him that there was a man in Lerwick called Jock Laurie who had three ice cream vans and was looking for someone to relieve one of his drivers for two weeks. Father took the bus to Lerwick the next day and returned with an ice cream van loaded with ten gallons of soft ice cream, something that had not been seen in Hoswick before. Within a few hours it had all been sold around Hoswick and Sandwick.

Jock was delighted with this and it wasn't long before events such as

Willie Smith in Jock Laurie's ice cream van, 1960s.   **Photo: Martin Smith**

the Sandwick Regatta and the Cunningsburgh Show had visits from his ice cream vans. The original two weeks went by quickly and father was asked by the other drivers to cover for them whilst they had their holidays. The two weeks became six.

At the end of the summer season Jock asked my father if he would be willing to work with fish and drive the company truck. Father needed the work and readily agreed to help Lowrie, Sonny, and young Lowrie Robertson sort and pack fish for shipment during the winter months. So began a working relationship that was to last 21 years and change all our lives, completely.

In 1962, Jock tried something completely new; he began to process brown crabs. This involved boiling the crabs and extracting both the brown and white meats. By now I was 14 years old and fed up with the prospect of nothing to do during the forthcoming summer holidays. Father asked Jock if there was anything that I could do in the factory.

About this time Jock, who was the type of man who would strive to find the answer to a problem, had been thinking about a means of extracting the meat from the crabs' legs, which were simply being thrown away. He had come up with the idea of using compressed air, so I was given the job of trying this out. It involved filling an empty Calor Gas bottle with compressed air then using this to blow the meat out of the crabs' legs. Modern-day health and safety regulations would not allow this to be done by a 14-year-old!

Over time various modifications were made to this machine – the final version had a foot-operated valve so that both hands could be used to feed in the legs and also the joints that connect the claws to the body of the crab. Three young schoolboys could each extract up to 40 pounds of meat in an eight-hour day using these machines. Naturally, this increased productivity and was much better than throwing the legs away. The meat from the knuckle joints had until then been extracted using the handle of a spoon.

It wasn't only crabs that we processed. Lobsters were being caught in such huge numbers that they were being boiled and broken up into their component parts as well. One problem was, again, the legs; they were at least two or three inches long, contained meat, and were simply being thrown away and the meat lost.

However, unlike crabs' solid legs, those of the lobster remain pliable even after cooking, and this was to be the key to solving the problem of how to recover the meat. Jock disappeared one day and came back from Home Furnishings with a Hoover washing machine and a roll of muslin.

Above: Shetland Seafoods crab factory, 1960s. Photographer unknown.

Right: The late George Hunter washing crabs for export to Sweden. Photographer unknown.

Left: Willie Smith with two fine specimens from Shetland Seafoods' lobster tanks. **Photo: Martin Smith**

We all wondered what he was going to do with them and we didn't have long to wait. Jock put a piece of muslin into the tub where the clothes normally go and then passed some lobsters' legs through the wringer on the top of the unit. The rollers on the wringer forced the meat out of the legs into the clean muslin – job done!

Using this method, the washing machine was paid for in three days; the rest of the season's production less the operators' wages was pure profit.

To give you some idea of the amount of crabs and lobsters being processed at the time, the following are the production figures for the year 1962-1963:

Year and Month	Brown Crab Meat	White Crab Meat	Roe	Lobster Meat	Monthly Total
1962	lbs	lbs	lbs	lbs	lbs
July	1458	1227	0	7	2692
August		738	252	1209	3167
September		793	434	1806	4104
October	3980	2136	161	780	7057
November	1390	979	200	980	3549
December	1706	1388	14	121	3229
Total for 6 months	10573	7261	1061	4903	23798
1963					
January	968	823	0	7	1987
February	1071	1214	0	0	3128
March	1868	1047	0	0	2915
April	3096	1530	0	41	4667
May	2926	1480	0	16	4422
June	4605	2527		957	8089
Total for 6 months	15566	8621	0	1021	25208
Total in lbs for 12 months	26139	15882	1061	5924	49006
Totals in kilos	11859.80	7205.99	481.40	2687.84	22235.03
Totals in tonnes	11.86	7.21	0.48	2.69	22.24

Shetland Seafoods' crab factory didn't only produce crab meat for Young's Seafoods. From time to time the factory processed crabs for clients in Sweden. The standard of food hygiene in Sweden in the mid-1960s was such that the following process had to be gone through:

1. Only female crabs were used.
2. Every crab had to have all her legs and nippers intact. They were then washed individually with a small high pressure washer.
3. The crabs were then boiled in herbs supplied by the Swedish client. (We had great fun getting those through customs!)

4. After boiling and cooling the crab's 'purse' was removed and if more than four drops of water ran out that crab was discarded and processed for the UK market.
5. The remaining crabs were then washed with the small high pressure washer again, ensuring that all the legs and nippers were still intact after washing.
6. A rubber band was placed round the legs and nippers on each side of the crab.
7. And finally, the crabs were vacuum-packed individually on to cardboard strips bearing the name of the Swedish company and the fact that the crabs came from Shetland.

Before the crabs could be exported a sample had to be taken to the council's environmental health department for approval. That done, and the necessary export certificate obtained, the crabs were boxed up and taken to Sumburgh where a private plane was waiting to take them to Sweden. Shetland Seafoods continued to export crabs in this way for a number of years. Lobsters were also exported, but usually live, which didn't involve any of the above procedures.

One disadvantage of working in the crab factory was the strong smell that got onto your clothes, your hair, even your skin. Of course, after a while we didn't notice it, but we soon became aware that there was something wrong when we went into a shop or, on a Friday, the bank with our pay cheque.

Sometimes, if there was a shortage of crabs and Jock's wife Winnie was busy with the housework, I made the Meadocream ice cream for the vans. The ice cream maker consisted of a large tank of brine with tubes of coolant running through it, and two rotating drums. The ingredients were put in and then a frame with two large blades, that just touched the sides of the drums, was lowered into each drum, the lids secured and the machine started up. As the brine cooled, the ingredients were stirred by the blades and also began to solidify and stick to the sides of the drums, from where they were removed by the blades. This mixing and solidifying process went on until the operator was satisfied with the consistency and taste of the ice cream.

You had to be careful not to allow the ice cream to get too hard, if it did it could break the blades. That meant expensive repairs, which couldn't start until the ice cream had melted again.

I wasn't the only young boy working in the crab factory during the 1960s, there were at least another four from the south end of Shetland. They were picked up at seven o'clock every morning by my father and me and taken to Lerwick. This meant we had to get up at 5.30am, have breakfast, and then set off for the Ness before driving to Lerwick. After a full day's work, and sometimes overtime as well, we had to make the return journey, often getting home to Hoswick at 8 or 9pm. This meant very long hours for everybody concerned. However, we were all young, fit, and eager to earn as much money as possible before going back to school or college.

The long summer holidays passed quickly, with a lot of fun along the way, and it left us all with some unforgettable memories. For example, the young men in question were, for the most part, under age to drive but they all had motorbikes. These had to be carefully hidden every morning before we set out for Lerwick in case the 'boys in blue' discovered them. On occasion, when we got to the pick-up point one or more of the boys would be missing. All we had to do to see if they were on their way or not was get out and look for the tell-tale blue smoke from the two-stroke engines!

I worked at the crab factory during two summer holiday periods – 1962 and 1963. Together with the others, I helped to put up plasterboard and tape and fill the joints in various extensions, and the new factory.

By now, the crab factory wasn't only employing local people but also some of the herring gutters who travelled up to Shetland every year to work for Joe Slaters, A. Wood & Sons, Pommer & Thomson's and W. Slater & Sons. These women were excellent workers and were able to work in the factory when there wasn't any herring to gut and pack. This suited both parties; the women made extra money and the crab factory could call on extra workers at a time of year when local labour wasn't readily available.

Before the 'Ness Boys' and me went back to school at the end of the summer of 1963, we trained the local women who were going to take over from us.

Jock and Winnie had three daughters – Sheila, Joyce and Shirley. They adopted a son, David, and fostered his older brother, Peter, and sister, Margaret. As the business grew it became necessary for Jock and Winnie to go south on business trips. One day Jock asked if my mother would come to Lerwick and look after the family while they were away. Mother agreed to give it a try and so we all moved into Jock's house at No. 89 King Harald Street.

The trial run went very well and this soon became a regular occurrence. As far as I was concerned, it meant an extra hour in bed in the morning, no waiting in the cold or the rain for the school bus, and being home again within a few minutes of the school day ending, instead of a bus journey to Sandwick.

Then there was the added attraction of fish and chip shops, cafes and the picture house, not forgetting Jock's extended family and their friends. It all added up to a complete change of lifestyle for me, one I very much enjoyed.

The crab factory was proving a hit and the products where selling well, so well that the family was being pressed into working there. Winnie found this difficult to do and run a family at the same time so it was suggested that my mother might like to relieve her from time to time. Mother's part-time job soon became a full-time one that lasted for 20 years.

Jock and Winnie Laurie.

Jock discussed with my parents the possibility of our moving to Lerwick. They realised that they had good jobs in the factory and that I would be leaving school soon looking for work. So it was agreed that, as one of Jock's key workers was moving to Aberdeen so that his wife could attend hospital there, Jock would ask Lerwick Town Council if they would transfer his 'key worker's house' to us.

Now, Jock was a very kindly man, and he was always holding out his hand to you with sweeties or sometimes money. One night, when he opened his hand, a Yale key fell into my mother's. "What's this for?" mother asked.

"That, lassie, is the key to your new hoose in Lerwick," was the reply.

Next day Jock took mother and father to see the house and we moved in a few weeks later.

On the day that we moved in, I went from Hoswick to school in Lerwick by bus as usual, but instead of going home asked one of my pals to take me to our new address – 34 Leslie Road. The door was open when we got there but there was no one in. My pal left me and, as I waited for my parents to arrive with our furniture, I walked round what seemed to be an enormous house, wondering how we were going to fill it.

The inside toilet together with hot and cold running water were major improvements. The crab factory and school were only minutes away and we had access to all the shops and other facilities that we could wish for. We settled into our new home and routine very quickly.

However, things could have become very difficult for us if the crab factory hadn't continued to prosper and my father had lost his job, because 34 Leslie Road was let to us on condition that, should he cease to be employed by J. & W. Laurie (later Shetland Seafoods Ltd), we had to vacate the property.

I have to admire my parents' courage for accepting this condition and making the move from Hoswick to Lerwick.

The Commercial Course

Having talked about going to school in Lerwick to take a commercial course in earlier chapters, the following details about the actual course itself should give you some idea of what we were taught and how it prepared us for our working lives.

Learning the three skills of shorthand, typing and bookkeeping, that made up the commercial course, was completely new to all of us in secondary 1C. When we got our first book of Gregg's shorthand symbols we might as well have been looking at the hieroglyphics found in Egypt for all the sense that it made. However, it wasn't long before we were able to write, and more importantly read back correctly, short sentences. Over time, our skill and speed increased to the point where most of us could write shorthand accurately at 100 words per minute. We checked each other's speed using a stopwatch.

Typing was another skill that had to be mastered from scratch. First of all, the typewriters were all heavy manual models, housed in great big desks with a lid that lifted up to reveal the machine. Considerable strength was needed to overcome the weight of the typewriter and the powerful springs that counterbalanced the whole unit. If you didn't get the system to lock properly, and let go at the wrong time, the desk slammed shut with a force that would have broken bones in young arms, fingers and hands had they got in the way.

Having got the desk opened, paper was inserted in the typewriter and a wooden cover placed over your hands so that you couldn't see the keys.

Next you had to find the 'home keys' – A, S, D, F, for your left hand and J, K, L,;, for your right. The space bar was operated with your right thumb.

On the wall at the front of the class there was a large diagram of the keyboard and, using this, you now started to learn to type: *aqa aza sws sxs ded dcd frf fvf ftf fgf fbf* with your left hand, usually a line of each sequence, and then, with your right hand, *juj jnj jyj jhj jnj kik kmk lol l,l ;p; ;/;*. You can imagine the racket in the classroom when over 30 machines were all doing the same thing at the same time!

Having managed the basic sequences you went on to simple words and then words and numbers and finally capital letters. These presented a particular problem because when you pushed down the capitals key the whole 'key basket' moved down to allow the large letters at the top of each key to reach the paper. This whole assembly was heavy and returned to its original position by means of springs. You used your little finger to overcome the springs and move the key basket so if you didn't apply enough force you finished up with what was known as flying capitals i.e. half a capital letter and half a small letter – I can't demonstrate this because modern computers don't do flying capitals!

Over the four years that the commercial course took, we progressed with our typing to the point where most of us could do 30 words a minute. There were several ladies in our class who could do a lot more than that. We were also taught how to keep the machines clean, change the two colour ribbons, and how to remove the ink and paper debris from the metal type letters using stuff that resembled Plasticine.

Typing was only the start; we had to learn all about the sizes of paper and envelopes, how to fold the paper, and what size went into what envelope.

In addition, we had to be able to 'centre' a document on a page, both left and right and top to bottom. This usually involved being handed a hand-written document and told to put it on either A4 or, as was more common at that time, foolscap paper. You started by counting the lines top to bottom, and then the characters in each line until you found the longest. You had to remember the number of spaces that there were across the page and how many lines were on a page from top to bottom. It was then a matter of working out where to set your left and right margins, and how many lines to turn up the paper before you started to type. There were NO fancy rulers to guide you, it was all done using your head and working it out on paper.

When you finished typing the document you folded the page right edge to left edge and checked to see that the type was all correctly lined up. You then repeated this by folding the bottom edge to the top edge, once again checking that the lines of type didn't overlap. If they did, you had to start all over again!

Columns of figures were another skill that had to be mastered. You had to set the margins and the 'tabs' for each column manually across the page. You moved from one column to the next by pressing the tab key. The carriage was returned manually to the start of each line, up-spacing one or two lines at a time depending on the spacing that you had selected using the line spacing lever.

From time to time we would be told to use one of the two 'long carriage' typewriters to do documents or lists with columns of figures. As the name suggests, the carriage was long enough to take foolscap paper on its side. These machines were widely used in solicitors' offices for preparing deeds, wills, etc. so it was essential that we all knew how to use them.

Just a few weeks before we left the school an electrically-operated typewriter arrived, and also what looked like a reel-to-reel tape recorder. It was, in fact, an early Dictaphone machine. We were shown how to operate both these machines because it was felt that it wouldn't be long before they began appearing in employers' offices.

We already knew how to dictate letters at a certain speed so that part was easy. It was also much easier to listen to the tape via headphones and type, as opposed to reading shorthand and typing. The Dictaphone tape could be rewound using a foot pedal, and a section repeated over and over until you were sure that it was right. With practice you could time it so that you hardly needed to stop typing to listen to the tape.

Our teachers, Jean Campbell and Margaret Sinclair, are to be congratulated for the excellent job they did in passing on to us the skills required for life in an office.

Our bookkeeping skills were taught to us firstly in class 1c by an elderly lady called Lena Mouat, who was replaced by Andrew Millar. Over the next three years we progressed from simple cash book entries right up to the preparation of profit and loss accounts and balance sheets.

It wasn't all hard schoolwork. From time to time there were episodes of light relief. For example, Mr Millar was a keen fisherman and one day asked if I would go to the canteen and collect half a dozen dessert spoons, take them to the metalwork room, and there remove their handles, drill a small hole in the wide end and several bigger holes over the rest of the spoon.

I agreed to do this but expressed concern at what might happen to me if I was caught nicking and destroying perfectly good spoons by either the cooks or the metalwork teacher. I was assured that they knew all about it and I would come to no harm

So I went first to the canteen where I was greeted by the head cook who asked if "I had come for Andrew's spoons." I said I had and was duly handed half a dozen that had seen better days.

I then proceeded to the metalwork room and was busy removing the handles when the teacher came in. He looked over my shoulder and said, "I see you got the job of making spoons for Andrew's fishing expedition."

I finished the job and no more was said about it by anybody. I just hope he caught some fish with them.

To give us a break from our commercial class work we got two periods of woodwork every week. When we were in our final year we were given the chance to make something that we could then buy for a small fee and take home. I decided to make a sledge and used an old desk lid, made out of good quality oak, suitably cleaned and shaped for the front of the sledge. The oak was fairly thick so I decided to carve my initials in the underside. I began by finding the centre and carving the middle letter, M.

A few days after I had finished doing this, Mr Millar asked me if, for a small fee, I would let him have the sledge for his son, Andrew. I could always make another sledge at home so I agreed to finish the sledge by carving the letter A in front of the M.

Prior to our final bookkeeping exam Mr Millar gave us several test papers to complete in the time allowed. The idea was to get us used to the kind of questions we might be asked, how to take time to study them, and plan how we were going to work our way through the exam paper. This was an extremely good idea because when it came to the actual exam, the paper was almost an exact copy of one given to us by Mr Millar just a week earlier.

The importance of one more skill was impressed upon us before we left; how to answer the telephone correctly. We were each allocated a day on which we had to answer all the incoming calls. The Central School had two numbers and when a call came in we had to answer it using the correct number, ask the caller how we could help, then mute the call and speak to the other party before putting the caller through. Muting the call was necessary in case the headmaster, for example, didn't want to take the call at that time, and obviously he didn't want the caller to hear that! If all went well you put the caller through, if not you had to apologise and ask them to call back later. These were live calls so you had to do it right or you soon got to hear about it!

About two months before we were due to leave the school we all had to go and see a careers officer. My interview took place on the top floor of Brentham House, at three o'clock on a Friday afternoon. I don't know about anybody else but I never saw or heard from the man ever again!

Just two weeks before the end of term I was sent with two other boys for an interview at the local office of an HM Government department. All three of us were interviewed on a Friday afternoon and told that they were only looking for one employee. We would be told on Monday which one of us had got the job. I'm sorry to say that, 47 years later, all three of us are still waiting for a reply!

After a week we wondered what to do and decided to go and visit our headmaster – the one and only George W. Blance, better known to all as Dodie Willie. We told him about our interview the week before and asked if he had received any reply. He said he hadn't and proceeded to look through some papers on his desk. After a few minutes he gave each one of us an appointment date and time with a local firm. I'm pleased to say that all three of us got jobs with the firms concerned.

Friday, 4th of July, 1964, was our last day at school and, not unnaturally, we had all been looking forward to it for some time. We spent time in the morning going round our various teachers and the cooks in the canteen, saying goodbye to them and getting their good wishes for the future, and their signatures on the back of our class photographs. The headmaster, Dodie Willie, visited all the classes who were leaving, congratulated us on what we had achieved during our time in his school, and wished us all the best in our chosen careers.

At one o'clock, our school days finally came to an end, we said our goodbyes to our classmates, and left. Instead of taking the usual short-cut, I took the long way home to 34 Leslie Road. As I walked, the euphoria of the last day began to wear off and my thoughts turned to the future. I knew I had spent the last four years doing the course that I had always wanted to do. I had passed my exams and I had a job to go to on Monday morning, but I couldn't help thinking "What happens now?"

The weekend passed quickly and soon it was Monday, 6th July, 1964. I got up early and, with a mixture of trepidation and excitement, got ready. My father gave me a lift to Alexandra Buildings where the firm of Lowestoft Herring Drifters Limited had their offices. I knocked on door number 5 and a voice shouted "Come in".

This was it – I was about to start full time employment!

To be continued...

Appendices

The Smith Family of Milltown 'Milton', Stove, Sandwick.

Father: Thomas John Smith

Mother: Joan Smith

Family: Joan: Never married; brought up 'Milton' after his mother died.

William: married Chrissie Smith.
Family: one son, Willie (deceased), (the author's father).

Margaret: married Stanley Sothcott.
Family: one son, Stanley Milton Sothcott. Margaret died of TB three months after her son was born. Her husband is believed to have married again and had another son.

Isabella Jane Malcolmson: married Laurence Harper.
Family: one daughter, Jane. Jane Snr died four hours after giving birth. Jane Jnr. (deceased), always known as Jean, was brought up by her aunt, Agnes Harper and her father. He died when she was just 12 years old.

Thomasina Barbara: married James William Thomson Henderson. Family: three daughters and one son (deceased).

Tomas John: married Laura Margaret Jamieson.
Family: one son (deceased) and one daughter.

APPENDICES 131

Pages from a booklet detailing HMS *Rangitata* – see chapter
Grandparents Sandwick

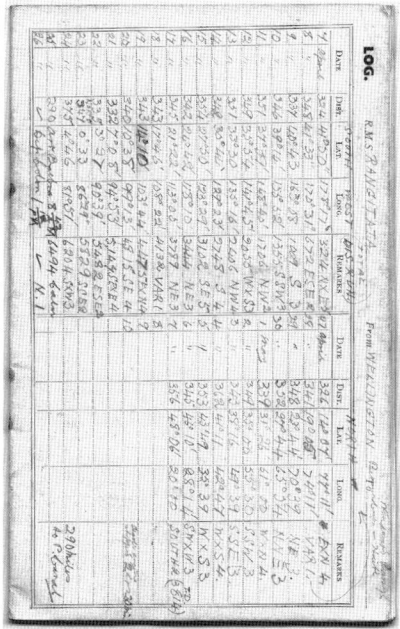

Extracts from a diary

Extracts from Willie a' Milton's diary, kept during his years as postman and caretaker of the Carnegie Hall. The words in brackets and /or italics are mine, inserted to clarify various points.

28/10/1950   Started with the Post Office.
21/02/1951   Rain and Gale – Soaked.
22/02/1951   Fine no coat
14/04/1951   Snowed all Day
26/04/1951   Fine – casted peats.
10/07/1951   Heaping Spuds.
11/07/1951   Dellin Crub 2 hours
29/08/1951   Rain Soaking *(There are numerous references to 'soaking' in the diary because, of course, they had no waterproof clothing of the kind available today.)*
27/10/1951   Total C.O.D's *(the customer paid the postman 'cash on delivery' of the parcel – no cash, no parcel)* for one year £773 2s 4d
25/12/1951   Christmas Day – Fine (all postmen worked on Christmas Day. Only New Year's Day was a holiday)
28/01/1952   Deep Snow mail late 25 bags
08/02/1952   Gale, Showery – Funeral Davie.
06/06/1952   Start holidays – very hot.
26/06/1952   End of holidays got 1 load of peats home and 1 load to the road.
28/06/1952   West becoming North East Cold – Tab Died.
29/10/1952   Total C.O.D's for 2nd Year £573 7s 1d
31/01/1953   Waiting time 5 hours, did half a delivery to 11 a.m. Gale 110 miles per hour.
15/06/1953   Close, rain – regatta day.
25/02/1954   Postmaster Visited.
10/06/1954   Got a load of peats home, built up and then cleaned hall. *(More about the hall later.)*
06/08/1954   Fine, finished barrowing peats – Biddel Died. *(Biddel lived in the old post office next door to Willie a' Milton at Rocklea. The first telephone exchange in Sandwick was in his house.)*
09/08/1954   Funeral of J. Work. (Biddel)

APPENDICES 133

03/11/1954 Bikes came. *(Very heavily-built bicycles with gears and a large tray on the front for the mailbag.)*
08/11/1954 Bikes Official.
09/12/1954 South East Gale – Walking Soaking. *(The bikes couldn't be used in strong winds; the heavy mail bags on the front made them unstable in the wind.)*
22/12/1954 Used Frank's van to finish off Christmas Mail Deliveries. Frosty with snow. *(The van belonged to Harold Frank Mathews who had a shop at Leebotten, so every effort was being made to get the mail to the public before Christmas. Don't know if the Postmaster at Lerwick would have approved.)*
25/12/1954 Christmas Day – Walking icy roads. *(Bikes couldn't be used on ice for obvious reasons.)*
15/01/1955 Blizzard – mail late.
19/02/1955 to 28/02/1955 Roads blocked no mail.
03/03/1955 First day Bike.
17/05/1955 Sunny with hail showers – at the hill – first casting. *(Peat cutting.)*
01/06/1955 Mail Strike at the hill raisin peats!
16/06/1955 Drizzle showers finished raisin peats.
28/10/1955 Five years with post office.
07/11/1955 Holiday Queen's Birthday.
26/12/1955 Christmas Mail more than average calls – fine.
28/12/1955 Walking, Gale, HELLISH.
16/01/1956 Gale, rain, soaking.
17/01/1956 Snow, icy roads, walking.
18/01/1956 Gale snow.
19/01/1956 Snow, icy roads.
20/01/1956 Thaw, soaking.
21/01/1956 Snow, icy, walking.
14/06/1956 Two air mails, wind north, hail showers, boat sunk!
16/06/1956 Started holidays, Sledging peats, fine and foggy.
17/06/1956 Regatta Day, Breezy fine for sailing. Rona and Thora won cups.
18/06/1956 Not much wind, Surf won both races, Sud Ayre second. Fine night for regatta concert.
23/06/1956 Two loads of peats home.
03/10/1956 Cut corn.
29/10/1956 Six years with post office.

24/11/1956 Gale with sleet – soaking
25/11/1956 Gale with sleet – soaking
12/12/1956 100 MPH Gale – walking – soaking.
21/12/1956 17 Bags Christmas mail
22/12/1956 26 Bags Christmas mail
25/12/1956 Christmas Day – South East Gale – Delivered Christmas Mail.
28/12/1956 Ship ashore.
30/12/1956 35 years married
05/02/1957 Hell of a gale – walking.
16/09/1957 Makies funeral.
08/10/1957 Got half a ton of coal.
02/11/1957 Got a load of peats home.
25/12/1957 Christmas Mail, Christmas Dance. Gale, Hopeless.
15/05/1958 Casting peats *(he was now 64 years old)*
08/06/1958 Saw Hamilton *(Dr. Hamilton)* got certificate. *(He was diagnosed with angina.)*
15/06/1958 Saw Hamilton got certificate.
22/06/1958 Saw Hamilton got certificate.
05/07/1958 Got peats home.

And what was probably the saddest entry that he made in his diary reads:
11/07/1958 The Milton roof fell in. *(This was the straw roof of the house in which he was born and brought up.)*

03/11/1958 Auntie's funeral.
25/12/1958 Fine. Christmas Dance.
11/04/1958 Casting Peats
26/06/1959 Bagging and Borrowing peats.
23/07/1959 Lumgair Funeral.
03/08/1959 Fishing 2 fish *(Probably the ling that I remember hanging up in his shed.)*
29/09/1959 Deliver election cards
22nd and 23rd October 1959 No mail for Noness, Curfield, Hillside or Houlland, the first time in 9 years that ever happened.
24/10/1959 Got dividend from pools from Flunkey. One Shilling! (5p)

And finally, after nine years as postman, he writes in his diary a draft of his letter of resignation.

To the,
Postmaster Lerwick,

Dear Sir,
I wish to tender my resignation as Postman at Sandwick (East Side) No. 57 as from Oct. 31st. If I have holidays to come, any time during October will suit me, you could let me know what time would be most suitable for you.

Yours respectfully,
W. Smith
Postman

A social evening was held in the Central Hall to mark the retirement of William Smith (Willie a' Milton). Mr Peter Tait made a complimentary speech after which a wallet of notes was presented to Willie by Miss Sylvia Leask. Patsy Bray sang *The Isles of Gletness* (I have been told that this may have been the first time that the song by John Barclay was sung in public.

Afterwards the following appears in his diary and also in the local paper:

On my retirement as postman I wish to thank the people of my postal district for the presentation made to me at a social evening in the local hall. Special thanks to Mr. Tom Halcrow the collector and Miss Sylvia Leask the presenter also to Mr. Peter Tait for his complimentary speech and to all who contributed to a very pleasant evening.
William Smith
Ex. Postman
Sandwick

Some pictures shown in the Carnegie Hall by the Highlands and Islands Film Guild (Geordie Horne):

1955
July 8th   Doctor in the House
July 22nd   The Kane Mutiny
Aug 4th   Happy Ever After
Aug 19th   Purple Rain
Sept. 2nd   Kit Karsen
Sept. 16th   West of Zanzibar
Nov. 30th   The Prisoner
1965
Oct 1st   The Longships
Oct 15th   Carry on Spying
Oct 29th   Four for Texas
Nov 12th   Carry on Cleo.
Nov 25th   Flipper the Dolphin

Library books issued in 1966:

January	71
February	125
March	98
April	94
May	128
June	130
July	108
August	174
September	75
October	167
November	156
December	99
Total	1425

Extract from *The Shetland Times* of 27th April, 1945, the day the author's parents were married:

Showing at the North Star Cinema: See Here Private Hargrove.

Adverts:

Wanted   Seal Skins
          Otter Skins
          Wild Bird's Eggs!!!!!

          Char Woman Hourly Rate 2s (10p)

Coal was rationed to 50 cwt in 12 months

Hosiery Buyers from Aberdeen, Glasgow, Surrey, Edinburgh, Cornwall and Lerwick advertised for supplies.

The Gilbert Bain Memorial Fund received the sum of £2 2s 6d from the Sandwick U. F. Church being part proceeds from lantern lectures.

Extract from *The Shetland Times* of 21st May, 1948, the day the author was born:

The film They Made Me a Fugitive was showing at the North Star Cinema.
Prices: Balcony Stalls 2s 6d Balcony 2s 3d Back Area 1s 9d.

Fish Report: In Lerwick 7 seine netters made 19 landings which sold for £305 and 2 great Line Boats landed 25 cwt which sold for £92.

At Voe 13 seine netters made 43 arrivals and landed 308 cwt selling for £738.

At Scalloway 2 seine netters landed 7 cwt selling for £23 and 1 great liner landed 9 cwt which sold for £65

Herring Report: good landings after a poor start. It was estimated that 51 local boats would be at sea by the 1st of June. These would be joined by up to 45 south boats.

There would be 13 Pickle curing firms in operation during the season 11 in Lerwick, 1 in Whalsay and 1 in Scalloway a total of 110 crews.

In addition there would be 2 Kippering operations an Lerwick and 4 in Scalloway plus 1 Klondyking, 1 Quick Freezing and 1 Meal and Oil.

Hosiery: There was a report on the proposal to free Shetland Hosiery from Purchase Tax with effect from the 1st of June. Buyers Anne Cane from London and Tulloch of Shetland advertised for supplies of Shetland Knitwear.